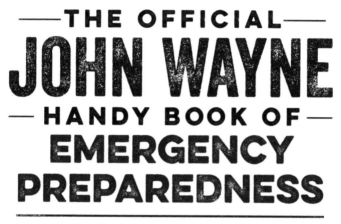

THE OFFICIAL
JOHN WAYNE
HANDY BOOK OF
EMERGENCY PREPAREDNESS

ESSENTIAL SKILLS FOR PREPPING, SURVIVING AND BUGGING OUT WHEN DISASTER STRIKES

**CHECK FREEDMAN AND
BILLY JENSEN, GREEN BERET (RET.)**

ILLUSTRATIONS BY DAVID PREISS/MUNRO CAMPAGNA ARTISTS
COVER ILLUSTRATION BY RICHARD PHIPPS

INTRODUCTION

 E LIVE in an increasingly unstable world. With social unrest, pandemics, natural disasters and other emergencies on the rise, you need to know you can take care of your own when things go sideways. But planning for disaster to strike isn't a last resort or 11th-hour task to undertake—there's a lot of ground to cover, and the best time to get started is well before you spot trouble on the horizon. The most well-prepared among us are those who can jump into action any time, any place.

Fortunately, we have a timeless role model to provide inspiration for life-saving success in the face of danger: John Wayne. Both on-screen and off, Duke was a hero to millions for his composure, his courage and his ability to protect himself and those around him when the going got tough. While these may seem like innate traits and abilities present only in heroes of the silver screen, they can all be learned and perfected by the average citizen. That's where this book comes in.

Inspired by John Wayne's iconic grit and informed by decades of elite training, this book has instructions and advice for mastering timeless skills that will help you prepare your mind, body and spirit for any emergency life might throw your way. Whether you need to defend your home from an intruder, build a shelter in the wild or survive an environmental catastrophe, these methods and techniques will help you ready yourself and those you care about for the tall task at hand. The world is full of enough known and unknown threats to instill fear in anyone, but the prospect of being unprepared for incoming disaster is undeniably scarier. As Duke once said, "Courage is being scared to death but saddling up anyway."

In 1953, John Wayne starred in *Island in the Sky* (pictured), an adventure film based on a 1944 novel of the same name by Ernest K. Gann that detailed the author's experiences rescuing downed airmen in the northern wilds of Canada. That same year, Gann published *The High and the Mighty*, a novel about a doomed flight from Honolulu to San Francisco. In 1954, Gann penned the screenplay for the film adaptation of his novel, in which John Wayne starred as First Officer Dan Roman, who's tasked with doing everything in his power to not ditch the plane in the Pacific Ocean.

Oliver Hardy
and John Wayne
in *The Fighting
Kentuckian*
(1949).

CONTENTS

Noah Beery Jr., John Wayne and Walter Brennan in *Red River* (1948).

THE PREPAREDNESS MINDSET

INCREASE YOUR
ODDS OF SURVIVAL
BY READYING YOURSELF
BEFORE DANGER STRIKES

PREPAREDNESS EXPLAINED

HE ART of preparedness can be summed up succinctly: It's all about decision-making. We make hundreds, even thousands of decisions every day, so we're used to thinking on the fly. But knowing how to best sort out our means of survival requires flexing a future-oriented decision-making muscle—the one that looks ahead and weighs the possible outcomes, hoping for the best while preparing for the worst. One way to do that is to develop a matrix for making decisions that will help unclutter your thinking and streamline your options. One such matrix, and one you'll see referenced throughout this book, is called the traffic light model. Most of us are familiar with the color-based signal system of a traffic light: red (stop), yellow (slow) and green (go). Using this same format, we can translate this tool into a methodology for conducting risk assessments.

Before we take any action of note, we must first conduct an overt risk assessment. This is something we do consciously and unconsciously, but when the action may be risky or have noteworthy consequences, we stop and take the time to assess the risks and any possible damage we could sustain, then weigh those against the potential gain.

The stoplight analogy is a fantastic tool because it is so easy to remember. Green is a go: Everything checks out and there are no glaring flaws or risk factors. Yellow is a risk factor: Two risks may be mitigated, but three or more yellows means a no-go. One red is an absolute no-go. One red means there is a potential risk that is simply too great to justify any potential gain or reward.

Thus, when planning, look for these indicators. If all is green, you have nothing to mitigate and you can proceed as planned. If you have one or two yellows, you must put

mitigation measures in place before you go, but once you do, you're off to the races. Three or more yellows or one red is a game-stopper. No-go. Back to the drawing board till you can get the proposed activity down to a green or at least two mitigated yellows.

Let's say you plan a long road trip. If you decide to leave after work on a Friday, the fact that you're likely to be tired is a yellow. If it so happens you have a cold and aren't feeling well, that's another yellow. The good news is you can drink some coffee to mitigate the first yellow and take some non-drowsy cold medicine to mitigate the second one. But if you had a terrible argument with your boss and you're worried about your job, that's a third yellow. Since three yellows can't be mitigated, you might want to change your plans, get a good night's sleep and leave the next day instead.

See how it works? Try using the traffic light model next time you're planning an outing, activity or adventure. You'll find it helps weigh decisions about risky actions logically and objectively and gives you an external unit of measurement to help you decide when you are unsure how to proceed.

THE OODA LOOP

OODA, a term common among those engaged in preparedness training, stands for Observe, Orient, Decide and Act. It is the process we go through in order to make an intelligent decision to ensure our actions bring about the desired results.

O - *Observe.* This is the part that usually gets short-changed, especially when timing is critical. In an active shooter situation, for example, we don't have all day to observe—we have seconds. We have to fly through the steps in the OODA Loop and get to the Act part because lives are on the line. In most situations in life, though, timing is not as critical. In fact, we usually have more time to observe than we actually take, so it behooves us to not be impulsive and spend a few more moments to formulate a rational assessment.

O - *Orient.* This is when you have observed all the inputs you can, and all that's left is to determine how those data points impact you individually and collectively. What is your position relative to your choices? For example, if you're lost and you pull out a map to help you get home, the very first thing you need to do (after recognizing you are lost) is to orient yourself. Observe the terrain and visual clues, then find that place on the map to gain a sense of both where you are and where you want to be.

D - *Decide.* Your observation and orientation give you data from which to make your decision. Is it enough?

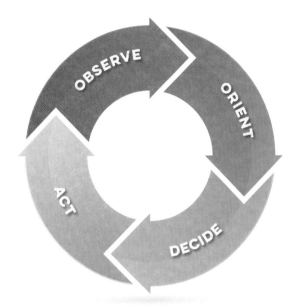

What happens if it's not? When people do not feel that they have enough data to make a good decision they naturally go back to the first step—Observe—then they move on to Orient. This is a sound plan, as long as you continue to move on to the next step: decide. Many times, people bounce back and forth without justifying or committing to a course of action, which is what's happening when someone freezes in fear. Don't let that happen to you: Find the point your data leads to and let that be your guide.

A - *Act.* You took in information, figured out how it impacts you and made a decision. Now it is time to carry out your decision.

Then what happens? You guessed it. Right back to step one: observe. That's why it's called a loop. As soon as you get through the last step, evaluate what you just did. That takes you back into observation mode.

An entire loop can occur in seconds or, in the case of something like stockpiling a shelter, it can take months. Recalling these steps can help clear confusion, calm chaotic thinking and slow the impulse to rush through things in a panic. Just knowing what your brain is up to can allow you to take control, shift your thinking and choose actions based on information rather than fear.

THE FULCRUM PRINCIPLE

Every person has a fulcrum upon which their balance rests. It comprises three parts: Physical, Emotional and Spiritual. Each of these three is equally important and, if any one of these is neglected, the entire person is out of balance. Each part must be invested in, protected and provided for in order to ensure a whole and healthy person.

Physical. Everyone needs food, sleep and exercise in order to survive. The trick here is having these in moderation. Eating is not all there is to food: A person's intake must be of nutritional value in healthy amounts. It does very little good to eat only junk food, just as it does very little good to eat only lettuce. Sleep is another input that must be moderated. Most adults have terrible habits at times, often staying up way too late before getting up way too early. Sleeping for 12 hours a day, however, is not beneficial, either. Exercise can be just as tricky. Some of us are gym rats who can't seem to work out enough for our own tastes, while others of us sit in the car on the way to work, only to sit in front of our computer for eight hours, to then come home and sit in front of the television until bedtime. We all need good quality food, sleep and exercise in healthy amounts in order to fuel ourselves and feel rejuvenated.

Emotional. It is important for us to do things that bring us happiness. That might look like pursuing a hobby, cultivating relationships by visiting with friends or family or serving the community in some fashion. We need to allow ourselves to spend a moderate amount of time on the things that help us relax, laugh, feel connected and feel useful in the grand scheme of things. Again, too much time spent here leads to an imbalanced fulcrum just as too little time does.

Spiritual. Everyone stands by a conviction, whether that involves a belief or a lack thereof. Whatever your beliefs, dedicate time to practicing them. Depending on where you stand, set aside time to pray, meditate, study, reflect, worship, debate, reason, learn and grow. Neglecting the practices and tenets of your belief system will also result in an imbalanced fulcrum.

If you prioritize your own fulcrum and invest time into all three categories on a regular basis, you will find yourself strong, resilient and ready to take on the challenges of adversity and emerge as a conqueror. This type of training, which doubles as living a healthy life, is called advanced preparation.

BUGGING OUT: WHAT IT IS AND WHEN TO DO IT

HE TERM "bug out" was originally a British military slang term referring to soldiers fleeing in a hurry, often in defiance of their orders. U.S. military forces later adopted the term, and it eventually found its way into our common vernacular. Bug out is now used to signify a planned emergency evacuation from a dangerous unplanned situation like a catastrophic weather event or violent civil unrest. Knowing an event could happen in your neighborhood and collecting the gear

QUESTIONS TO ASK

- Am I healthy, fit and strong enough to handle the rigors that always accompany bugging out?

- What are the risks if I stay vs. if I go?

- Do I have all the supplies I need if I stay? If I go?

- Is there any chance there will be a mandatory evacuation order?

- Is the danger going to overtake or surround my house?

- If I leave, will I be going someplace safer than here? Once I get there, how will I survive?

- Can I carry my bug-out bag for miles on foot by myself?

Paul Fix and John Wayne leap into action in *Back to Bataan* (1945).

and supplies to see you through an evacuation is where the planning occurs.

How do you know when it's time to go? Answering that question is easier when you use the traffic light risk assessment (see pg. 8) and the fulcrum principle (see pg. 12).

Your answers will determine the initial choice you make, and that choice may change as the situation unfolds. Whether the situation is dangerous weather, a biochemical spill, a riot or some unholy confluence of all three, situations are dynamic. Do not stay married to your first decision. Continuously evaluate and re-evaluate the situation and be prepared to change your mind when the situation reaches your personal decision threshold.

POTENTIAL BUGGING OUT BARRIERS

Preparing for an emergency means preparing for potential problems with your escape plan, too. Any number of obstacles could arise while you're in the midst of bugging out, but you can prepare for some of the most common challenges that could occur. The best thing to do is to turn on your TV or radio to a local news station. The federal Emergency Alert System will interrupt the regularly scheduled programs as often as needed to update you on the situation. It is set up to do so as soon as 10 minutes after a national disaster. This will be the way to find out about issues such as local road or bridge closures and figure out a work-around. As you listen to the news reports, keep a paper map of your area on hand to identify an acceptable detour. After you head out, continue to listen for updates on the radio as you go. For instance, if you are in the Florida Keys and there is a mass evacuation due to an incoming hurricane, you will find all inbound lanes of traffic (southbound) are temporarily reversed and the entire highway is being used for outbound (northbound) traffic to accommodate the increasing volume of cars. In any type of emergency, if you get stuck and cannot leave, take cover and find shelter.

THE LEGALITY OF BUGGING OUT

The United States does not have federal laws regarding bugging out, which is why it's crucial to familiarize yourself with state and local laws. The two topics most likely to be of concern are trespassing and stealing. Read the signs and signals: If you see "No Trespassing" signs, hear large dogs and see barbed-wire fencing, go somewhere else. You don't want to get yourself into a situation where the owner shoots first and asks questions later. Plus, the owner of the land will have a stronger case to prosecute if they have signs posted conspicuously. And whether it's a business or a residence, stealing is always illegal. It's always better to offer a barter than to simply take what you need as there are no special laws that allow you to steal in a crisis. The laws apply even during a disaster, but the court system will often take the emergency nature of the act into account. It's important to keep in mind that "emergency" means someone's life or physical well-being depends on what you do.

If you want to be able to receive and transmit data while you're on the go in a bug-out situation, the best course of action would be to get an FCC amateur radio license and a radio. Licenses come in three classes: Technician, General and Extra. This will allow you to both listen and talk to others who are trained, licensed and equipped to provide assistance in such cases. If you have a two-way radio, you can monitor 121.5 from anywhere in the country. This frequency is nicknamed "Guard" and it is an emergency-only channel that is used in the air, on land and on the water. It is designed to transmit distress calls (maydays), but you can also monitor this emergency channel to listen to what is being said by other individuals using it in your local area. But remember, this is strictly a broadcasting station—it will not provide news. You should return to your local news station about every 10 minutes to be sure you aren't missing any important updates.

PREPARING THE BODY

LL THE bug-out purchases you make and other details you've carefully considered won't do a lick of good if you cramp up after hiking half a mile with all your gear. Being prepared for an emergency includes stocking up, sure, but just as important a concern is bulking up. Knowing your body can handle danger is at least half the battle. There's no telling which physical challenges you may face in any given disaster. Circumstances may demand you run fast, lift heavy objects and perform other feats of strength as you navigate whatever challenges that emergency brings. Prepare accordingly.

OPTIMIZING YOUR CAPABILITIES

If you are a skier, you already know that in order to be in control during your descent of the mountain, your body must be in the forward center of gravity position, or forward CG. That is the most efficient, effective and controlled way to get down the hill. If you are forward CG as you ski and you hit an icy patch, it may throw you to center CG and you can quickly recover without losing your momentum, which is pretty ideal, all things considered. If you are center CG when you hit that patch of ice, however, it will throw you back to aft or rear CG, and you will fight harder to recover while losing some momentum. Not the best if you're in a race against time (or someone else), but still not the worst. That said, if you are aft or rear CG when you hit the ice, it will throw you down, stopping all your momentum and perhaps requiring external help to get you back up. This last scenario is what you need to avoid at all costs.

John Wayne puts up his dukes in a production still from *Conflict* (1936).

QUESTIONS TO ASK

- What is my current level of fitness?
- What sort of fitness regime would my doctor recommend based on current age and physical condition? (Never start working out without input and recommendations from your doctor.)
- What are the measures I should work toward to achieve my optimal level of bug-out fitness?
- What are the unique challenges on my property or in my area I might have to overcome?

The point of getting your body ready is so that you can hit any crisis in the forward CG position. In order to do so, you must ask yourself what you want to be able to do when a crisis reveals itself. For example, if you can't do a pull-up in normal times, you will not be able to do one in a crisis, either (after all, adrenaline can only do so much). There is no magic list here in terms of physical fitness goals to hit, but there are a few good places to start. Though there is no way to know in advance which type of crisis may unfold, there are some universally useful actions—running, fighting, lifting and hiding—that will prove helpful in nearly any emergency situation. To that end, train in a way that helps you improve your ability to perform those actions. A good format to use is called run/fight/run. That means get on the treadmill or the trail and run for 10 minutes, get off and "fight" (shadow box, hit the heavy bag, hit the speed bag, practice kicks, etc.) for 90 seconds, then go back to running. When emergencies happen, run/fight/run is the sequence of events you are most likely to find yourself in. Be sure to throw some weight lifting into your workout routine along with your cardio, and don't forget to find ways to practice hiding as well, especially when you're winded and have a hard time staying silent.

Marsha Hunt patches up John Wayne in *Born to the West* (1937).

PREPARING FOR YOUR LIMITATIONS

Since we're only human, it's possible you may already have a physical, psychological, financial or similar limitation or two to consider as you plan. Maybe you tore your ACL while playing on the varsity team in high school, or maybe you're a veteran learning to navigate civilian life with PTSD and unexpected loud noises trigger flashbacks. Or maybe money's tight right now and stockpiling supplies for an emergency sounds like a major investment. It's easy to get discouraged when we're focusing on the negatives, but be reasonable in your expectations of yourself. This is the time to determine workarounds that fit your personal circumstances.

If you have a back issue, for instance, and you can't lift more than a few pounds without needing to reach for an ice pack, simply take the time to divide your

KNOW YOUR WEAKNESSES

A bug-out situation isn't any time to let vanity get in the way of survival. Even the biggest and toughest among us have limitations, and denying them as we prepare for the worst can prove fatal. That's why it pays dividends to think ahead.

Are your hands less than steady under pressure? Invest in some head lamps to avoid a shaky flashlight. Any limps, lumbagos or other limb issues that flare up? Make sure your stock includes a lightweight, collapsible walking stick to keep you moving smoothly as you navigate tough terrain. If you're flat-footed, do your shoes have ample arch support? If not, now's the time to invest in a pair that accommodates your needs, or find the right inserts that will do the trick. How often do you rely on over-the-counter medication to manage minor aches and pains? See if you can go without it for a time.

The important thing is to be honest with yourself and plan for your weaknesses as well as your strengths.

provisions into smaller groups, then move them to your storehouse area one item at a time. If money is an issue, spread your purchases out over a long period of time. Watch for sales and use coupons. Research which brands are the best value for the price. Balance a sturdy product with the sticker price. Look for more expensive items secondhand, or check with places that deal in overstock. If your life depends on that piece of gear, get the best one you can afford. Get a second job with an outfitter and take advantage of employee discounts. Choose food and gear items that are force multipliers: For example, since you can make countless recipes with potatoes (which can keep for up to two or three months), stocking up on those in their various forms is like buying a multi-tool without the added sticker shock. See what you can whip up with few ingredients.

Whatever your limitation, the cavalry may not come, so it's up to you to handle things yourself. Invest in your strengths and determine workarounds knowing you might be the only one carrying out whatever

John Wayne and
Kirk Douglas in
In Harm's Way
(1965).

needs to be done. Sure, your workaround may take
more time than you anticipated, but if you have the
mental resilience to accept that your way is going to
be different but equally effective, you can accept the
slower speeds by keeping your eye on the goal. Moving
at a slow and steady pace is always better than refusing
to race.

PREPARING THE MIND

HE MODERN world offers so much convenience that sometimes it feels like we don't have to figure anything out on our own anymore. But in an emergency situation, your access to the internet, TV and even basic electricity can be compromised. Do you have the knowledge and wisdom to devise solutions to emergency situations without outside help? When adversity strikes, you'll want to be able to keep your wits about you, so stop scrolling through your socials and get to work building a better brain.

EMBRACING A CALM MINDSET

The best-laid plans can fall apart in a heartbeat when we let panic take the reins. Panic is when we abandon logic and reason and allow unthinking instinct to take over—when we catch ourselves reacting to events instead of carrying out objectives. In most cases, our instincts are designed to keep us safe. However, when dealing with panic, the things our instincts drive us to do can get us killed in the blink of an eye. Calm, the antidote to panic, can be just as contagious.

When you choose to keep calm during a moment of crisis, you exude cool-headed focus to the people around you, who in turn notice you aren't letting yourself be emotionally manipulated by the event. This helps them maintain their calm, too. Calm people are looked to as leaders in dire situations. In order to ensure this outcome when everything breaks bad, you have to train in advance. Rethink your relationship with fear by doing something that scares you every day. Push out of your comfort zone and stretch your limits. Learn to find your rhythm in stressful and scary situations.

John Wayne is ready to make tough calls in *The Green Berets* (1968).

John Wayne, George "Gabby" Hayes, Ella Raines, Ward Bond and Emory Parnell in *Tall in the Saddle* (1944).

Your capacity to handle them calmly will grow in direct relation to your level of exposure.

Practicing daily meditation or cultivating mindfulness is another good way to train your brain to not immediately throw itself into an emotional spiral when confronted with stressful stimuli. Volunteer for a job you find a little overwhelming and practice remaining calm when you notice your stress mounting. Exercise while doing breathing drills in order to control your heart rate.

Give yourself a stress inoculation of sorts by willingly placing yourself in a situation with a problem that must be solved and overcome. Calm will not automatically come to you when things are falling apart, but if you train it into yourself, it will be there when you need it.

Whenever negative emotions inevitably arise in response to your environment, it's important to give yourself the space to process them rather than ignore them. Show yourself empathy and actively listen to your train of thought as you talk yourself through what happened. Refrain from "should've, would've, could've" thinking, which is just another way to beat yourself up. Give yourself the time to acknowledge each thought or feeling as it comes up without letting it overwhelm you—you can name it, write it down, say it out loud, whatever you prefer—then imagine letting it go. It may sound counterintuitive, but examining your feelings is what keeps them from dominating your life.

QUESTIONS TO ASK

- What are the ways in which I handle stress? Are those healthy? What coping mechanisms can I employ to manage or lower my stress levels in moments of crisis?

- Who can I turn to for sound advice should I need to reach out for guidance?

- Who or what depends on me? How can I ensure those people, animals or things are taken care of in the event of an emergency?

- What have I done today to ensure my home and family are protected tomorrow?

- How can I practice mindfulness and incorporate it into my daily activities?

- What are my worst-case scenarios? What potential situations do I need to mentally confront in order to know I can take decisive action when necessary?

- What drills do I need to run with my household?

Steve Forrest (center) looks on as John Wayne (left) and Stuart Whitman (right) play chess on the set of *The Longest Day* (1962).

SEEKING OUT MENTAL STIMULATION

In a survival situation, keeping your mind busy is critical to ensuring your survival. Having someone to talk with, a book to read or a game to play can keep you sharp, relieve boredom and increase morale. As with our muscles, our brain grows stronger and more capable with use. The more we demand of it, the more it gives

YOU CAN KEEP YOUR MIND SHARP IN MANY WAYS

- Do math in your head instead of reaching for your calculator.

- Play the memory game: Look around you in every setting, taking note of every detail you can, then quiz yourself later on what you remember. Aim to recall a greater number of data points each time you play. You can also do this with items: Arrange your favorite handheld tools on a table in a certain order and give yourself 10 seconds to memorize the scene. What do you remember seeing, and where was it in the lineup?

- Play the what-if game by asking yourself what you would do if such-and-such happened. You are only limited by your own imagination.

- Write an original story or compose a song in your head. Make up a different ending to a movie.

- Pen a poem. Play an instrument. Learn to read music. Pick up a new language. Try a new recipe or make one up that's all your own. Take yourself away from your mental comfort zone and growth will follow.

us. When we become mentally lazy, our abilities begin to atrophy. This can be a gradual and insidious problem because people often fail to recognize the ground they are losing until, say, they're stranded in the wilderness, desperate for drinkable water but cannot remember how to make a solar still.

PREPARING THE SPIRIT

 HERE'S AN old saying that remains as relevant as ever today: There are no atheists in foxholes. You can prepare for a potential disaster by attending religious services, and it's here that you'll develop a spiritual support network. This can be of great help during an emergency, not only spiritually but also physically. Determine the most reliable people in your spiritual network, and when you meet to discuss issues of a spiritual nature, consider using that opportunity to get on the same page regarding disaster preparedness as well. The spiritual community can be one of your most reliable support systems in the face of catastrophe, but you'll be in even better hands if you're all on the same page before disaster strikes.

QUESTIONS TO ASK

- Do you consider yourself spiritual or religious?
- How do your beliefs—religious, spiritual or otherwise— impact your daily life?
- Do you tend to panic when you can't control a situation, or are you generally able to gain composure?
- What are some spiritual (or other) practices that reliably bring you peace of mind?
- Do you have a place you routinely visit that helps you feel more connected to your community and/or your belief system?
- Who are some like-minded people in your community you feel you can count on in an emergency?

Robert Mitchum and John Wayne head to church in *El Dorado* (1966).

INVEST IN SPIRITUAL PRACTICES

Do you believe in something? Act on it. Go to the services at your place of worship and listen to the teachings. Pray. Read the holy writings or scriptures. Give charitably. Act on the tenets of your faith. Meditate. Celebrate the holidays if you have them. Make time for your spirit. This invisible part of you is just as important as the rest of your makeup. You will not be truly forward CG unless all three parts of you are solid.

CONNECT WITH OTHERS ABOUT YOUR CORE BELIEFS

You might be tempted to think upholding your beliefs in private is enough to feed your spirit, but you'd be missing out on a critical social element that's often undervalued in our highly individualistic society. All human beings, on some level, require companionship, and practicing our beliefs is one of several ways we connect with others.

Talk to your clergy and the other members of your faith. Tell a close friend about what you believe and how you practice it. Ask them about their beliefs in a respectful way and they might share as well. Attend festivals, parties, celebrations, weddings, funerals, holiday gatherings, concerts and services. Serve someone or something outside of yourself by volunteering. Engage in respectful debates with like-minded people and people who think otherwise. Make friends. Share in their successes and trials, hopes and fears. Have people over for meals. Nothing feeds the spirit more than realizing you are not going through life alone, that there are people who are just as inquisitive, doubtful, hopeful or enthusiastic as you are. Faith practiced in a vacuum is the hardest road, so tread carefully and take the time to circle back to people with whom you share common ground.

SEEK SOMETHING
BIGGER THAN YOURSELF

Life is chaotic enough when things are going smoothly, so when it comes to managing your peace of mind, it pays to get in touch with the ways in which you can strengthen your spirit. But what if you don't attend church or practice religion? Can you still prepare that invisible part of yourself for an emergency scenario? Of course you can. Spirituality and religion are not synonymous for everyone. If you're not a religious person, the key to spiritual success is identifying the sources of calmness and comfort that help you feel connected to the world at large. There are many ways in which you might achieve this, such as volunteering at local events or establishments in your community, attending a meditation retreat or even just getting in touch with nature by going hiking or camping with a group of friends. Whatever it may be, you'll know you've found something worthwhile when an act or practice begins to make you feel rejuvenated and more at ease in your daily life. Spiritual strength doesn't have to come from a "higher power," if that's not what you believe in. You can find it by simply looking at the world around you with an open mind. So when disaster strikes, you can take solace in the fact that you are connected to something greater than yourself. No one wants to feel alone in an emergency situation, and no one has to.

SURROUNDINGS

 F YOU hope to make it through an emergency successfully, awareness of and ability to work with your surroundings are going to be of the utmost importance. If you're in the open when disaster strikes, how can you find or make shelter? If you're indoors, how can you make sure your environment is a safe one? Are there items around you that can be used to employ some of the skills you've learned from this book? If you can answer these questions with confidence, you're starting off on the right track.

SHELTER

While a house is the first thing that comes to mind, your shelter could be your shed, garage, shop, office, tent or any place you happen to get caught in when a moment of crisis arises. What people don't immediately consider is there are several levels when it comes to the concept of shelter.

The first level of shelter is the clothing on your own body: Your pants, shirt, jacket, coat and anything else you're wearing are the last line of defense against the elements. If you get caught outside with no possibility of getting indoors, your clothing just became all the shelter you have.

The next level up from clothing is a tarp, poncho or some other material you can hang over your head to keep the sun and rain off of you. The next level up from that is a tent that protects you on all four sides, as well as overhead and underneath. From there, shelter is a solid structure like a cabin, shed or detached garage, and, last of all, a home of some sort. It doesn't matter if it's a mobile home, an apartment or a single-family home, so long as it's set up for human habitation. Depending on your life experience, you may already

Jimmy Lydon and John Wayne in *Island in the Sky* (1953).

know how something like an RV can look like a palace to someone who has had to do without.

Ideally, you'll want to have myriad options for shelter that span the range of these levels. The important things to consider as you put your plans in place are the kinds of temperatures and weather events you are likely to encounter in your geographic region.

VEHICLES

Vehicles are not one-size-fits-all, so in the event of an emergency, it's likely that whatever you already have will do just fine. A vehicle is not just transportation—it can be your shelter, temporary home, storage unit, medical treatment facility, casualty collection point and link to the outside world via the radio. Different vehicles have different capabilities, but if you're in the market for one as you read this, here are some things to consider.

Trucks excel at hauling things, are generally workhorses, can take quite a beating and still run and have a flat bed you can use to sleep in, transport or treat wounded people and even bring in that eight-point buck.

SUVs are good in that they're also rugged and many have overland (off-road) capabilities, which can come in extremely handy if the need to truly disappear arises. This also gives you more accessibility to the exact spot where you plan to make camp.

Cars (sedans) do one thing very well: They blend in. You can lose one car in a sea of other cars, so if you ever need to maintain anonymity, that's easily

John Wayne and
Louise Latimer in
*California Straight
Ahead!* (1937).

MANUAL VS. AUTOMATIC

Ideally, you'll be able to use your own vehicle in a crisis, but
that's not guaranteed. What if the only ride available has a
stick shift and you have to take the wheel? Will you know what
to do? This space is far too small to teach you how to operate a
manual transmission, but you should consider learning how to
operate different vehicles. Step outside your comfort zone and
practice driving stick or operating a motorcycle or ATV. Or, get
your boating license. The more feathers in your cap, the more
confidence you can have in a pinch.

accomplished. Cars can also fit into places trucks and SUVs won't, like garages, small parking spots and narrow streets.

Each vehicle type has its pros and cons, so whatever you have will work very well for limited applications. The good thing is all of them can function as a roof over your head, protection from the elements and a platform for rapid evacuation. After all, sometimes you have to make do with what you have.

NAVIGATING EMERGENCIES IN YOUR CAR
Disaster doesn't wait to strike while you're secure at home. Follow these tips to stay safe when you encounter trouble on the open road.

- Should you encounter a tornado, get out of your car and seek solid shelter at or below ground level. Tornadoes pick up cars and fling them around violently. This is a life-threatening situation, so don't attempt to outrun the tornado.

- Whether you come across a flood or a downed power line, stay put in your vehicle, as exiting can lead to drowning or electrocution.

- In an active shooter situation, put the engine block of the car between you and the shooter. The engine block will have more stopping power for the incoming bullets than any other part of the car.

- During a blizzard, stay in your car. Keep the exhaust pipe clear of piled-up snow to ensure no fumes make their way back into your vehicle, which can prove deadly. Wrap yourself up in the space blanket from your cache of emergency survival gear. Keep the heat on. Eat the energy bars in your kit. Flash the headlights every so often to signal for help. Listen to the local news station for updates.

- In the event of a volcanic eruption, stay in the car and drive away from the lava flow. Be prepared to drive on the metal rims if the lava pops and melts the rubber tires.

ITEMS TO HAVE IN YOUR CAR

If you find yourself in an automotive bind, you can rely on the following hacks to get you to point B safely and in one piece.

- Use toothpaste to clean the headlights and restore them to the brightness necessary to drive in the dark.
- Remove rust and corrosion from the battery with cola (Coca-Cola works well). Remove the battery, pour the soda on slowly and watch rust dissolve. Dry and replace the clean battery.
- For a very short-term solution, replace a broken section of hose or pipe with an empty Pringles can and some duct tape.
- Use a piece of chewed gum to stop a liquid leak like fuel, oil, brake fluid, coolant, etc. Make sure to clean the outside surface of oil, dirt and debris to ensure the gum will stick.
- Keep bottled water and emergency rations in your car alongside a full toolbox.
- If you cannot get traction on a sandy, snowy, icy or muddy surface, stop spinning the tires. Get out of the vehicle and place something on the ground that will separate your tires from the slick surface like boards, cardboard boxes, rocks and pebbles, cat litter, sticks and branches, etc. You can keep a commercial product called Tire Socks in your vehicle for ease of use. Build a "road" from underneath the tires to where the ground is hard enough to drive on. Accelerate slowly to maximize traction.

SECURITY

YOUR SHELTER is ultimately only as useful and safe as it is secure, so make sure you know how to lock things down well before the need arises. A good old-fashioned alarm system is a good place to start, but remember, you might not be able to rely on emergency services to respond to the alarm, so be ready to make do on your own. You'll want to board your windows, barricade your doors, make sure you have an escape plan in order and prepare yourselves to defend against any potential danger. But the legwork doesn't stop there. Read on to discover how you can evaluate your home's defenses and patch up the weak spots when it comes to encountering natural and man-made threats.

ALERT NETWORKS
Security is a huge concern in the mind of someone aspiring to be prepared for anything. There is a lot to consider. The most foundational security consideration begins with your relationships with

QUESTIONS TO ASK

- How many doors are there and where are they?
- How many ground floor windows are there and where are they?
- How can I reinforce the doors and windows, add locks or place barricades to prevent them from being opened by force?
- Are my windows candidates for shatterproof coatings?

John Wayne, Harry Carey and Gail Russell in *Angel and the Badman* (1947).

the people geographically closest to you, like your neighbors. Now is the time to invest in those relationships. Strike up a conversation. Learn people's names. Be courteous, respectful and helpful. Surprise people with kindness. Deliver homemade cookies, if that's your thing. Look out for their interests. People will remember your kindness or your unkindness and it will come to mind when they are in a position to benefit you or harm you. Picture the idea of your security like a series of five concentric rings with you

John Wayne in
Ride Him, Cowboy
(1932).

at the center. The first, closest ring consists of the members of your own household. After that, there's your next-door neighbors, followed by the rest of the people on your street or in your building, your neighborhood and finally your town.

If you want people to look out for you, help you in your time of need, keep your best interests at heart and let you know if they discover a possible threat to your safety, you must treat them in such a way that you build social capital with every interaction. In short, if they like you and appreciate your kindness, they will look out for you. If they don't, it's more likely you'll have to go it alone.

FIREARM SECURITY TIPS AND TACTICS

Security is not something that happens to you based on your circumstances or a series of random events. It's something you constantly pursue, research and practice. If you have a firearm and you plan to use it for home defense, how often do you train with it? Do you have a plan for how to maximize its capabilities during a moment of crisis?

- **Never point the gun at anything you are not willing to destroy.**

- **Never put your finger on the trigger until you are ready to pull it.**

- **Always keep the gun pointed downrange.**

- **Always know what is behind your target.**

This is pretty straightforward stuff, all things considered. But do you always know what's behind your target? Furthermore, do you know what kind of damage your particular round will cause? Will your target stop the round, or will it go right through? Will

RESPONSIBLE GUN OWNERSHIP

The key to responsible gun ownership is getting the appropriate training in the use of your own firearms. Keep your skills up to date through consistent practice at home and at the range. It does no good to purchase a firearm and put it away for an emergency without acquiring the training, skills and proficiency to use it effectively. We all owe it to the human beings around us to be trained, capable and safe with our gear in any situation. You can practice at home by dry firing with an electronic target and by conducting drills of your household's emergency plans. When you go to the range to practice live fire, go with a training plan and use the time wisely to increase your skill level and stay sharp. Practice defensive shooting and not just marksmanship by drawing and firing from a holster, firing around an obstacle or running low light and no light scenarios where you have to illuminate the target with a flashlight while firing. Choose a setting that allows you to practice firing at a moving target. Aim to put in as many real-life complications as possible to prepare for what might happen in an emergency.

it go through drywall, doors or furniture? Is there a possibility it will ricochet? Do you know who's on the other side of that drywall or door if the round does go through? Is your target backstopped by true cover or by concealment alone? How many sectors of fire do you truly have in your own home (concealed within easy reach) when your children are in bed? Where are your pets? How effective is your lighting? Where will that bullet travel if it goes through your wall and out of your house?

The answers to these questions are crucial to home defense. Walk around your house, inside and out, and meticulously note the answer to all these

Fuzzy Knight and John Wayne in *The Sea Spoilers* (1936).

questions. Once you've finished, build a plan that factors in all of those answers, then memorize it and rehearse it regularly. Run exercises. Practice like your lives depend on it. Know the firearm laws in your state and precinct. Once that round leaves your gun, you own it and all the damage it may cause.

WHAT TO STOCK

A gun requires ammunition of the correct caliber and type. For self-defense ammo, you'll want hollow point (rounds that flatten out on impact) or frangible rounds (rounds that break apart on impact), which are designed not to go all the way through the target so they minimize the risk to everyone else. Ball ammo, sometimes referred to as range ammo or full metal jacket ammo, is not the right choice for personal or home defense because it goes right through humans and out the other side, meaning it could potentially hit an innocent person. How much ammo you want to stock is a personal and financial choice, but a good rule of thumb is that it should be enough to last through a home defense encounter such as a burglary. Ammunition needs to be kept dry and reasonably cool, so be sure to throw some desiccant into the safe with it.

A responsible firearm owner also requires a gun safe to store firearms and ammunition in such a way that no unauthorized person can access it. A biometric or quick access safe is good for accessing the gun in one second flat when needed while keeping it secure at all other times. If you are going to go that far, a high-quality flashlight, mounted to the gun or not, is a must-have for low light operations. A red dot and a laser can be added to the package to help you aim faster and with more accuracy. A high-quality knife worn on your non-dominant side can be a great help in weapons retention in the event you get into a life-or-death struggle for your gun. These are all options you'll want to consider as you take stock of your home defense capabilities.

GUN SAFES

The most secure way to store your firearms—whether from children or unwanted visitors—is in a gun safe. These devices can also protect their contents from weather-related damage from fires and floods, so you'll have the peace of mind that should you need to reach for your firearms, they'll fulfill their purpose. High-tech options are available, if biometric scanning is your thing, but combination locks, keys or multi-lock safes will do the trick just fine. Ultimately, you will need to decide what best fits your budget according to your needs, so weigh your decision carefully.

QUESTIONS TO ASK

To help narrow down your options, you may want to ask yourself:

- How big does the gun safe need to be to accommodate all my firearms and ammunition?
- Where do I intend to put it?
- Can I bolt it or otherwise secure it to the floor to make it impossible to steal?
- How quickly do I need to be able to access what's inside?
- Do I want an additional safe closer to my bed so I can have faster access in the middle of the night?
- Am I willing to be dependent on electronics and batteries or do I want a key or combination safe?
- Do I need the speed that comes with biometric access?
- Do I need more than one safe?

DEFENDING YOUR HOME

When an intruder breaches your security and breaks into your humble abode, you have more strategies at your disposal than staying hidden and hoping the police will arrive in time—especially if you've got firearms. Learn how to best defend your home and survive an encounter with an unwelcome visitor.

A TRUE BACKSTOP A solid brick wall or even a bookcase can stop a bullet and are considered cover.

BETTER SAFE Keeping your firearms in an easily accessible (but beyond the reach of children) gun safe is the best way to ensure you have what you need when you need it. A safe in the master bedroom is good practice—as is a backup firearm in an office or side room.

DRYWALL ISN'T A BACKSTOP Just because you're seeing a wall doesn't mean it'll stop a bullet. Firing toward interior walls that aren't solid is a major risk.

AREA OF FIRE A safe area of fire takes into consideration the path your bullet will travel. While firing on an intruder as they step through your front door might make sense in the moment, if you miss, the bullet could travel to a neighboring property.

EVERYDAY CARRY

VERYDAY CARRY, or EDC, is a phrase referring to the things you carry on your person on a daily basis. The list works both at home and abroad. However, you must familiarize yourself with the local laws in order to decide what you are allowed to carry where. Laws vary from country to country, state to state, county to county and town to town. Know the laws and do not carry anything illegal in any locality.

By now, you understand the concept of surviving out of your clothes, fighting out of your gear and living out of your pack. This means that you need to keep anything necessary for your survival in your pockets and on your person. You need to be able to handle the situation out of your purse, backpack, messenger bag, etc. Dress for the baseline and the climate. Have a baseline-appropriate head covering with you, even if it is not always on your head. It can help you change your look quickly. Keep eyeglasses or sunglasses with you for the same reason. Dress in layers so you can shed, reverse or relocate pieces quickly. Choose your shirt and pants to be flexible, comfortable, rugged and filled with as many pockets as possible. Concealed carry shirts with hidden pockets and cargo pants are optimum. Again, remember the baseline of your locality. Shoes must be comfortable and rugged for walking, running and fighting.

Keep a jacket with you. It's a versatile item that won't just keep you warm—it'll also help you change up your appearance in a flash if you're being pursued, and its pockets provide extra storage. It can be tied around your waist, slung over your arm or stuffed in a backpack whenever you're not wearing it. It can function as a bag, a tourniquet and even a weapon, in that it extends your reach and allows you to swing something at your attacker's face as you attempt to disengage, but it can also work as a method of concealing something. Perhaps you have something valuable you don't want stolen from you like a purse or a medical kit, something that denotes your faith like a Bible or a Quran, or something that people wouldn't approve of you having, like a self-defense weapon.

Ideally, you should also have pockets in your shirt and pants. You will need to find a methodology for distributing your tools across your pockets. When you find a configuration that works for you, be consistent. You want to know where each thing is without thinking when the moment of adversity strikes.

A knife has many routine uses. It should be easy to access but not alarming to anyone who happens to see it—just be sure to check local laws to see what kinds can be carried in public.

A tactical pen functions primarily as a pen, so it should also be kept in a location that's easy to access. Tactical pens are usually made out of steel, aluminum or titanium. They can function as a stabbing, pressure point, trapping or joint control weapon. They often come equipped with a glass breaker, and some models include a multi-tool, flashlight and whistle as well. Yours should at the very least have a glass breaker. As a simple pen, they are allowed in most buildings, but they are a powerful weapon to anyone who takes the time to learn and practice the necessary skills.

Button compasses are pretty small these days. They can be clipped to just about anything non-metal. If you get a well-respected brand like Suunto, it will be every bit as reliable as a full-sized compass. This tiny device can help direct you to safety.

Paracord is the most amazing tool in existence. Consider keeping a small amount (about 10 feet) on you. It comes in 550, 750, 850 and more.

John Wayne in
Angel and the Badman
(1947).

Those numbers represent pounds of tensile strength. Be sure to get good quality paracord so it can do whatever you need it to do.

A lighter is also a tool with daily use as well as tactical use, so keep this in a place where you can access it easily. Remember its unconventional use in an avalanche (see pg. 208)?

A bobby pin is the Mighty Mouse of tools. It has many uses and can be easily carried and concealed. Unlike other critical preparedness items, it's not illegal anywhere and you'll never feel it in your clothes. These little gems can be turned into lock picks, shims, screwdrivers, clips, leads, antennae, conductors and more. There's no good reason not to carry one, two or even three on you.

A cell phone can be your one-stop shop for getting yourself rescued, finding your way out of a mess, receiving or researching new information or providing time-critical data via voice, text, photo or video, depending on your model and plan.

Most people like to rely on their cell phone for the time, but there is good reason to wear a watch. So long as it isn't flashy, there's no need to conceal it and it takes up zero pocket space. It's useful all day long and never gets in the way. Knowing the time is an incredibly valuable piece of information. Being able to time things is also a necessary capability. If your phone is lost, stolen or broken, you'll still need a way to handle these things.

If you are in an unfamiliar area, get a printed map. If you should need it, the map and the compass will be your ticket home. Just don't be obvious about referencing it in public places if you're looking to keep a low profile.

Firearms are a personal choice. Open carry. Concealed carry. Brand. Size. Caliber. Having one on you can make you an incredibly hard target, but do not become myopic. You are carrying many tools. Some are for survival. Some are for fighting. Some are for escaping or even avoiding a bad situation. Use all the tools available to you and always prioritize in this way: Avoid. De-escalate. Escape. Evade. Defend.

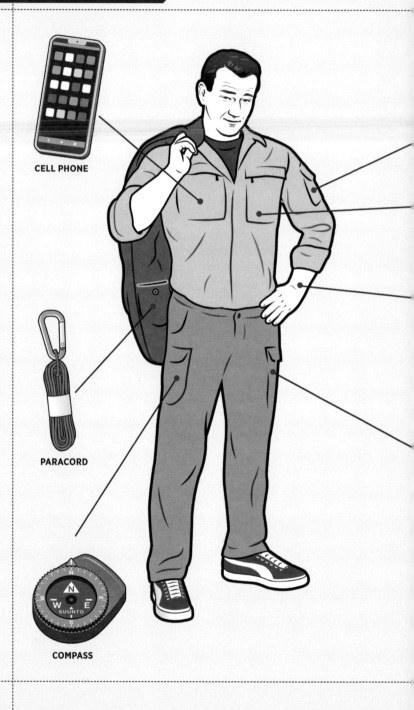

CELL PHONE

PARACORD

COMPASS

TACTICAL PEN

BOBBY PIN

POCKET KNIFE

LIGHTER

WATCH

ITEMS TO CARRY

You'll want to keep these incredibly handy force multipliers on your person at all times. You might even get creative with a few of them. For example, a lighter can be a signal, while a tactical pen can break through glass or be employed as a weapon. Employ these essential items to orient yourself, defend yourself—whatever the situation calls for.

MAP

John Wayne in
*The Sons of Katie
Elder* (1965).

SHELTERING IN PLACE

KNOW HOW TO DEFEND AND MAINTAIN YOUR HOMESTEAD WHEN STAYING PUT

SHELTERING IN PLACE

HELTERING IN place has many advantages. For starters, you're typically in your own home and have access to all your possessions. You don't have to worry about how much something weighs, how much space it takes up or whether you can carry it for any great distance. You can stock generously and resupply from your own stores. You can be comfortable, with access to all your clothes and your own bed. You can access your entire book collection to pass the time or—presuming you still have power—put on your favorite John Wayne film. But sheltering in place has some drawbacks too. If you do not take the time to stock the provisions you want to have in the event of an emergency, it'll be too late when something happens, which means all you'll have on hand is what you thought to grab the last time you were out. And that's usually not going to cut it in an emergency scenario.

The key to enjoying your shelter-in-place experience is in the advanced preparation, which starts by visualizing what you might need if leaving wasn't an option. The experience created by the conditions brought on by COVID-19 makes imagining being stuck at home for weeks on end a little easier. Consider stocking extras of things like soap, shampoo, deodorant, toothpaste, mouthwash and other everyday toiletries. Running out of hygiene products will become both a health and a morale issue in a very short amount of time. Choose a length of time for which you want to be prepared to hunker down, then do a little math to figure out how much of each provision you would go through in that time. Again, your experience during COVID can be instructional here: There was a time

John Wayne in *Flame of Barbary Coast* (1945).

folks thought they'd have to fight each other for toilet paper, but in the end, wish they'd stocked up on stuff like ibuprofen. Buy 1½ times the amount you think you will use in case you spill some, give some away, barter with some or wind up sheltering in place longer than anticipated.

MEDICAL CONSIDERATIONS

S NOTED, one of the best things about sheltering in place is you don't have to worry so much about the weight of your gear or how much space it takes up. A basic first aid kit might be all you have room for if you bug out, but when you're planning on sheltering in place you can make a closet into a respectable med tent if you've got the room. Doing so starts with an understanding of what you might need and why.

BURNS

A burn is a special kind of wound and requires special treatment. Burns can be caused by multiple factors, including electricity, hot water, chemicals, fire, a hot stove, an iron, steam, etc. Since burns will swell, it is important to remove any clothing or jewelry from the site immediately. If the clothing or jewelry is burned into the wound and fused together with the skin, do not attempt to remove it. That requires a hospital.

If the burn is from a dry chemical, leave it in its dry form and brush it off your skin and clothing. Always brush away from the body, being careful not to spread the chemical around. Launder the clothes and take a shower, running cold water over the burn for 30 minutes.

WHAT TO STOCK

- ☐ Burn gel
- ☐ Burn pads
- ☐ Gauze
- ☐ Medical tape
- ☐ Pain medication
- ☐ Salt
- ☐ Silver sulfadiazine cream

If the burn is not from a dry chemical, remove the surrounding clothing and jewelry and hold the burn under cold running water for 30 minutes. Do not use ice: You can compound the problem by freezing the burned tissue, which will result in frostbite. After the heat of the burn has been significantly reduced, apply burn gel and cover it with a burn pad. Tape the four sides to the skin outside of the affected area, then wrap it loosely with gauze. Do not impede circulation.

Regardless of the cause, if the burn is particularly bad, you can help it heal by rehydrating the skin twice a day.

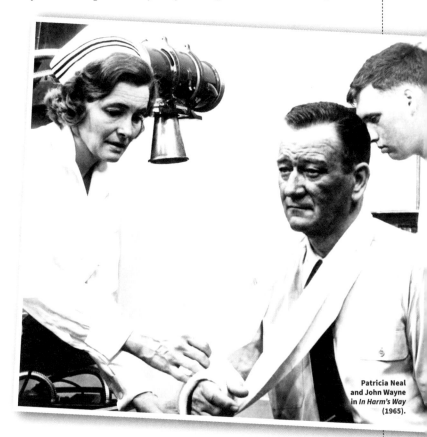

Patricia Neal and John Wayne in *In Harm's Way* (1965).

Use salt to make a simple saline soak of 1 percent salt and 99 percent water. Soak the burn in the simple saline for 10 minutes twice a day and the skin will rehydrate by osmosis. After soaking and gently drying the burn, apply silver sulfadiazine cream directly to it, cover it with a burn pad, tape the sides down and wrap it loosely with gauze. Burns can be tremendously painful so be prepared with the necessary medication on hand.

BREAKS AND SPRAINS

Breaks and sprains need to be immobilized while they heal. In a situation where you can get to a hospital, splint the affected area just the way you found it without manipulating it. In a situation where you cannot access a hospital, you may need to straighten it in order to treat it. This is the least desirable option. In either case, having a pair of crutches or a sling on hand will go a long way toward keeping you comfortable and ambulatory. A SAM Splint is malleable and can be molded to the affected area, after which you can attach it by wrapping the area in an elastic bandage. Check for blood flow in the fingernails or toenails downstream from the injured area to ensure it is not too tight and circulation is good. Not sure? Just pinch the nail and let it go and see how long it takes to go from white to pink. If it takes longer than three seconds, the circulation has been impeded.

In the event of any sprain, be prepared to take some pain medication. Rest, ice and elevation of the injury will be key for the first 48 hours.

WHAT TO STOCK

- ☐ ACE bandages of varying sizes
- ☐ Crutches
- ☐ Pain medication
- ☐ SAM Splints of varying sizes
- ☐ A sling

HOW TO TREAT BROKEN BONES

Injuries can make an emergency even more of a challenge. When the going gets tough in the realm of broken bones, you'll want to know how to keep things from getting worse until you can get to a hospital.

If you have medical splinting material like a SAM Splint, use that. Otherwise, you can use Popsicle sticks, tongue depressors, newspaper, magazines, pillows, jackets, camp chairs or just about anything else you have on hand that fits the bill.

To get started, simply wrap the affected area in the material at hand, then use duct tape or strips of cloth to hold it in place. Note: Do not squeeze the affected area while you wrap! This could make things worse. The desired outcome is to protect and support the break until the hospital can apply a proper cast. Splint the affected area exactly the way you find it without attempting to straighten it and evacuate the injured person to a hospital.

If the affected area is on a limb, include the joints above and below the break in the splint and immobilize the whole thing. However, if there's a reason you can't leave the affected area in the orientation you found it, straighten it slowly and gently to avoid causing more damage, splint it and evacuate to the hospital.

In every case, check for a pulse below the break and assess their capillary refill in the fingernails or toenails on the limb that's broken. To do this, pinch the end of one of their fingers or toes for five to 10 seconds, then release. Ideally, the end of their digit will regain its normal color in less than two seconds. If it takes more than two seconds, the person is probably dehydrated or experiencing limited blood flow. Either way, you'll want to seek medical attention immediately.

DO NOT attempt to align bones that are misaligned and/or attempt to put bones or anything else that comes out of a person back inside their body. These are serious medical procedures that require specific training and certification to carry out.

CHILDBIRTH

If you're in an already-fraught emergency situation and an expecting mother in your party goes into labor, you're likely to be a little stressed. But there's no cause for alarm. Childbirth was done in homes long before it became an automatic trip to the hospital and need not be categorized as a life-threatening emergency. However, in the event there are complications, be prepared to call for higher medical help.

When the time comes, make the mother as comfortable as you can. Prop her up with pillows, give her cold water or ice chips if she wants them, massage her head and shoulders and stand by with a bowl for potential vomiting. Speak calmly and reassuringly and encourage her efforts. There is no guarantee about how long it will take.

WHAT TO STOCK

☐ A clean string

☐ Heavy maxi pad

☐ Medical gloves

☐ Plastic bag or container

☐ Sterilized trauma shears or scissors

☐ Washcloths and towels

With medical gloves on, position yourself between the mother's legs and be prepared to assist or even to catch the baby as it is delivered. Tie a string tightly around the umbilical cord 4 inches from the baby's belly button and another one 4 inches from the mother's. Use the sterilized trauma shears or scissors to cut the umbilical cord between the two ties.

Clean the baby and the mother with wet washcloths and hand the baby to her, wrapped in a blanket or a towel. Use the towels to soak up all the fluids and apply a heavy maxi pad to help contain the continued bleeding. Keep the placenta (afterbirth) in a plastic bag or container so the hospital can run lab tests on it once the mother and baby make it to a medical professional.

Mildred Natwick, John Wayne, Harry Carey Jr. and Pedro Amendáriz in 3 Godfathers (1948).

Give medication for pain or nausea as needed. Wash or throw away the bedding and towels. Take the mother's and baby's temperatures every couple of hours to ensure they are both doing well. Offer ice packs and heating pads to the mother. Stand by for diapering the baby. Let them rest.

HOW TO CARE FOR A NEWBORN BABY IN AN EMERGENCY

If a pregnant member of your household or group goes into labor, you're going to need to learn how to keep that precious bundle of joy alive once they've been delivered.

Establish a schedule for eating, sleeping, bathing and cuddling and stick to it as closely as you can. Babies thrive on schedules—it brings them a sense of calm, peace and security, which translates into a well-adjusted temperament. Try to keep the ambient temperature comfortable and constant and have lots of layers of clothing and blankets around to enable you to make micro adjustments. Sing softly to maintain an atmosphere of peace. It may sound counterintuitive, but don't tiptoe around a sleeping baby. Instead, make a normal level of noise so they learn to sleep more and startle less. Talk to the baby to form a bond and stimulate their brain activity. If you need to argue with someone, do so out of the baby's hearing. Aim to create an atmosphere of security and safety.

In terms of basic needs, breastfeeding is optimally designed for the baby's health, but this only works if the mother can eat enough food and actively keep her stress level under control to be able to produce milk (if breastfeeding is an option—no shame if not). If you don't have disposable diapers on hand, stock up on cloth diapers, which you can also fashion out of clean flannel sheets, microfiber towels and the like. Keep baby acetaminophen on hand in case of pain or fever. You'll want to bathe the baby three times a week—more than that and you could dry out their sensitive skin. You can stock wipes designed for waterless sponge baths, which will help you keep the baby clean and healthy even without running water. Keep Desitin diaper rash cream on hand for the baby's comfort.

As a rule of thumb, choose the most secure room in the house to be the baby's sleeping quarters. In the event of a home defense situation, it'll be the first place you go, so make it count.

John Wayne in
3 Godfathers (1948).

Wilfrid Lawson, Moroni Olsen, Claire Trevor and John Wayne in *Allegheny Uprising* (1939).

ILLNESS
If you have a medical issue requiring prescription medication, make sure you keep a good supply of it on hand and have a plan for obtaining more. Outside of that, keep a well-stocked pharmacy at home to treat anything you can think of such as an upset stomach, heartburn,

HOW TO SET UP
A QUARANTINE

Should you or a member of your household get sick, you'll need to devise a way to let them heal while keeping everyone else safe. The way to do that is by setting up a quarantine.

If you're at home when disaster strikes, you may need to designate a quarantine area, which includes a bathroom and sleeping facilities for anyone who needs it. You can deliver food, drink, medication, books, games, toys and whatever else the infected person might need by leaving them outside the door, knocking to announce the delivery, then retreating so they can retrieve whatever you left for them. You'll want to wear disposable gloves when you go back to retrieve dishes or anything else you need to clear away to keep germs at bay. Dispose of the gloves each time you handle anything the individual in question handled and always wash your hands.

If you need to have contact directly with the quarantined person, wear a disposable mask, disposable gloves and eye protection. To keep your risk of contracting their illness low, you'll want to minimize your contact time regardless of whether it's an airborne or direct contact disease.

As always, if possible, try to seek medical attention. A quarantine takes discipline to maintain, especially when it comes to long-term care. If you decide to set one up, be sure everyone sticks to the rules you've set. Don't deviate from the plan.

WHAT TO STOCK

- ☐ Acetaminophen (Tylenol)
- ☐ Activated charcoal
- ☐ Antacid (Pepcid, Tums, etc.)
- ☐ Anti-congestion (Sudafed)
- ☐ Anti-diarrheal (Imodium)
- ☐ Anti-nausea (Pepto-Bismol)
- ☐ Aspirin (Bayer)
- ☐ Bacitracin
- ☐ Betadine
- ☐ Cortisone
- ☐ Cough suppressant/ expectorant (Robitussin)
- ☐ Diphenhydramine (Benadryl)
- ☐ Electrolyte solution (Gatorade, Jigsaw, Liquid IV, etc.)
- ☐ Ibuprofen (Motrin, Advil)
- ☐ Iodine
- ☐ Magnesium
- ☐ Milk of magnesia (Phillips')
- ☐ Muscle rub (Icy Hot, Bengay, etc.)
- ☐ Naproxen sodium (Aleve)
- ☐ Potassium
- ☐ Prescription medications
- ☐ Styptic

cough, congestion, muscle cramps and aches, headaches, fever, allergies, nausea, etc. Most of these medications have a good many years of useful shelf life so if you buy a big bottle of each it will last you quite a while. It's a good idea to get used to not taking medicine for every little disturbance in your system when you're not dealing with an emergency condition so you can weather the storm if you don't have everything you need exactly when you need it should things go south. Returning to the idea of building layers of security, you might want to have enough of these types of supplies on hand, especially the lighter and non-perishable items, to share with your neighbors if they get caught without provisions and have a need.

OTHER MEDICAL CONSIDERATIONS

For cuts, scrapes, bleeding, bites, stings, infections and other sorts of potential at-home injuries, you can round out your medical kit by adding the items on this list. It is one thing to have the supplies on hand but that does not help you until you know how to use them properly. If you haven't taken a first aid, wilderness first aid, CPR or stop-the-bleed class, there's no time like the present. Reach out to your local firehouse or EMT station for more info on classes in your area.

HOW TO TREAT A FEVER

A fever is a common sign of illness and happens when the body is fighting an infection. It might be extremely unpleasant, but it's not necessarily a terrible thing—it's simply the body doing what it was designed to do in terms of staying healthy. However, there are times when the body cannot overcome the cause of the fever on its own, and you'll need to know when it's time to get help.

It's possible you may not know the underlying cause of how the fever came to be. It might be the product of an infected wound, a bite or sting, an illness, a heat injury, an allergic reaction or something else. The underlying cause will determine the level of risk, so rack your brain or ask questions if you're treating someone else in your group.

If the fever is not accompanied by worrisome symptoms such as a headache, stiff neck, nausea, shortness of breath, etc., the person in question may not need to take any medications. Simply getting out of direct sunlight, resting and hydrating may be all that needs to happen. If those symptoms begin to show up, you can treat the fever with acetaminophen or ibuprofen. Let them rest for a bit and check on them frequently. Most fevers break within a few days.

The threshold is usually 102 degrees Fahrenheit. If the fever gets that high and does not improve with rest, hydration and medicine, it's go time: Evacuate to a hospital immediately. A high fever can cause seizures and death, so move quickly—it's a life-threatening emergency that requires medical attention.

SANITATION

HEN YOU are sheltering in place, you have to think about how to handle normal things in a familiar setting in an abnormal, unfamiliar way. You may not have electricity or running water. You may not have heating or cooling. You may not have lights. That doesn't spell the end of everything but does mean it's the end of the old way of doing things. You need to think creatively. You may need to boil water before you can ingest it. You may find yourself using more hand sanitizer as opposed to water. You may have to take sponge baths instead of showers. You may not be able to rely on your refrigerator or freezer to keep your food safe for long periods of time.

Personal hygiene is paramount to your physical and mental health. Wash or sanitize your hands as often as possible. Clean your ears well after they have been in water, especially fresh water sources like lakes and streams, which are more prone to carrying disease. You can put a few drops of isopropyl alcohol into them to dry them out and kill bacteria. Only brush your teeth with boiled, purified, filtered or sanitized water. Eat all the food in your refrigerator and freezer as quickly as you can to avoid food poisoning.

PLAN AHEAD

If your freezer has the cubic footage, you can prepare for the worst by filling in any empty spaces with full 2-liter plastic water jugs. If you lose power, the frozen water bottles will extend your frozen food's life span by turning your freezer into an old-fashioned ice chest.

WASTE DISPOSAL

If the power goes out, such as in an electrical grid failure (see pg. 226), the toilets will cease to flush. Depending on the nature of the emergency, the waste

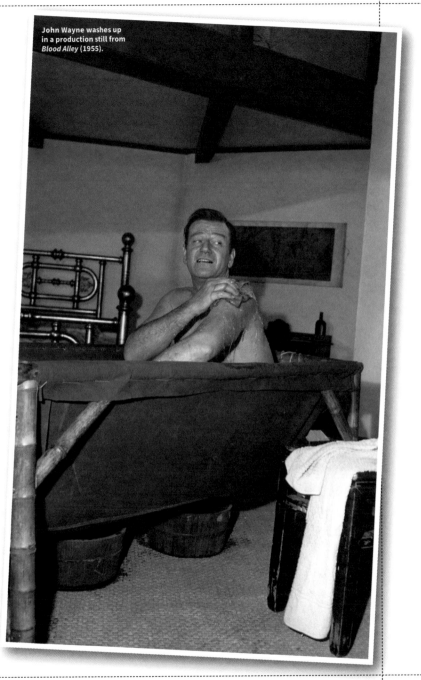

John Wayne washes up in a production still from *Blood Alley* (1955).

collection agency upon which you likely now rely to pick up your trash may not come. You may be on your own as far as maintaining a healthy environment where you're not surrounded by your own waste and refuse as well as the pests, bacteria and (let's face it) stench modern-day waste management helps us avoid. There are ways to deal with these issues.

In the bathroom, you can carry water to your toilet and fill the tank by hand each time you flush. If the bowl and the tank are both full they should flush normally. They may not refill on their own.

Additionally, now would be a good time to familiarize yourself with the nearest waste collection facility like a dump, incinerator or landfill. You may have to transport your own trash there every few days. Keep your outdoor trash covered with an animal-proof lid. Take the indoor trash out of the house and place it in the outdoor receptacle in heavyweight, industrial-strength trash bags. Close the lid and wait until that container is filled. If for some reason you cannot take it to the dump, you may have to bury it or burn it. This is only an option if you have your own property in a rural area. It will not work in cities or towns. If you do bury it, you will need to dig a hole twice as deep as the pile of trash, dump the trash in the bottom, fill it in with dirt and pack it down tightly so animals can't dig it up. If you burn it, make sure to do so in a safe place like a metal 55-gallon barrel. Keep the fire under control. Use jet fuel (you can buy Jet A at most municipal airports) to get as hot a fire as you possibly can. Do not burn anything that will put toxins, chemicals or poison into the air. Bury the ashes.

EVERYDAY HYGIENE ITEMS YOU'LL WANT TO HAVE ON HAND

Maintaining personal hygiene is paramount on every day ending in Y, but depending on the type of emergency you face, these items might be harder to find. That's why it pays to evaluate your household's needs and stock up ahead of time.

Your shopping list should include (but is not limited to):
- Baby powder or talcum powder
- Betadine
- Deodorant
- Dry toilet paper
- Hand sanitizer
- Iodine
- Isopropyl (rubbing) alcohol
- Pantyliners
- Peroxide
- Soap
- Wet wipes

MORALE AND BOREDOM

OW MORALE and boredom go hand in hand. Busy and productive people generally have a more positive outlook because they are fulfilled. If morale becomes an issue, there are some things you can do to infuse it with life. The highest of all callings is to serve someone or something outside yourself. Immerse yourself in meeting the needs of others. It crushes boredom and bestows fulfillment. Organizing tasks, coordinating people and resources, facilitating communication, constructing a shift schedule and rolling up your sleeves to do the grunt work are all excellent ways of rendering service. Real leaders serve. This is a kind of fulfillment that people in military service can take comfort in daily. By accepting a similar mindset in an emergency, civilians can do the same.

GAMES AND BOOKS

Since you might not have electricity, it is important to stock up on things that can provide entertainment and brain stimulation without requiring any power. Board games, novels, coloring books, origami paper, arts and crafts supplies, paints, stencils,

WHAT TO STOCK

- A travel chess or backgammon board or other travel-sized board games
- At least two decks of cards, preferably waterproof
- Books or magazines
- Crossword books
- Hoyle's *Rules of Games*
- Pens, pencils and paper
- Transistor radio and extra batteries
- Trivia games

John Wayne and his wife Pilar enjoy a game of gin rummy.

how-to books, newspapers, physical games (think Twister), cards, toys, reference books, textbooks, scriptures and a familiarity with games like charades and Pictionary are just a few examples of things to have on hand. And when in doubt, a trusty deck of playing cards and a copy of Hoyle can go a long way. If you have a family, make sure you have something for every age range so you don't start to lose the cohesiveness of the group. Lots of people come up with ideas for their own games and there is no better time to figure out the rules than when you have copious amounts of unaccounted-for time. You can even direct and perform a play for your family or neighbors. Just be positive and use your imagination. Don't fancy yourself a screenwriter or poet? Recall the plots of a few of your favorite John Wayne movies. Who knows—you might be hunkering down with someone who hasn't seen one or three.

FITNESS EQUIPMENT

If you have a weight bench, a BowFlex, a TRX System or a Roman chair, you're in luck: None of those require electricity. If you don't, you can put together a comprehensive workout area for a no-electricity situation with some simple gear. Physical fitness is as important to morale as combating boredom. It also keeps you occupied and engaged and allows you to maintain your level of readiness for whatever may come. Strength, speed, agility, balance, flexibility, stamina, endurance and power are all important to your health.

A large rubber ball like a Pilates ball has numerous applications including replacing your desk chair. A heavy punching bag, boxing gloves and a mounted speed bag allow you to work on your combat skills and stamina at the same time. Resistance bands can help with strength training and can also help rehabilitate an injured joint. Free weights like dumbbells and kettlebells allow for a variety of weight lifting configurations. Even your own body weight can be used: think push-ups, planks, sit-ups, stretches, isometric exercises and more. A pull-up bar

John Wayne and Pilar at home with their children, Aissa and Ethan.

mounted on a door frame allows you to work on upper body and core strength. If you have the freedom and safety to go outside for walks, runs, bike rides, football and Frisbee games, you can integrate those too. Just be sure to prioritize your physical fitness.

PROJECTS AND CHORES

Projects and chores have probably never seemed like a survival tactic before, but they are. When you need structure, mental stimulation, entertainment, physical fitness and morale, there is nothing quite like taking action to improve your quality of life. Consider *The Swiss Family Robinson*. In the novel by Johann David Wyss, the shipwrecked family could have sat on the beach with a signal fire, hoping for a rescue. Instead, they decided to start improving their position right away. They identified and tackled tasks, projects and chores, which resulted in a tree house and eventually all the comforts of home on an uncharted island. The nice thing about projects and chores is they elevate the well-being of the whole community. Chores contribute to sanitation and waste disposal, which in turn contributes to the health of the environment and its inhabitants. Cooking meals and doing other kitchen chores is always fulfilling when it's time to eat. Projects can be anything at all, like going into the woodshop and building something you've been wishing you had or making your own radio setup like the Professor on *Gilligan's Island*. You can inventory, sort, organize and categorize medical gear for quick response capabilities. Working out for the simple sake of physical fitness is fine, but you can use physical labor as a force multiplier when it accomplishes something, makes you strong, eliminates boredom and improves morale all at the same time. Start with a few minutes of physical activity every day and try to up your exercise by five minutes every day until you're spending about 45 minutes working out.

THE IMPORTANCE OF ORDER

Order brings peace. The state of our surroundings can influence our mental state. If we allow disorder, clutter and dirt to accumulate, it will take its toll on our mental space and erode our sense of well-being. Cleaning and organizing your surroundings is the first step toward reclaiming your sense of peace and composure. Declutter and deconstruct the piles of stuff. Put things away where they belong. Clean the dirt out. Our feelings are supposed to be the caboose on our train, not the engine. Don't let them lead you around. Decide to lead them by taking the actions that contribute to your serenity. Even in the best of times, our tranquility is threatened by the invasiveness of bad news and worries. Put yourself in the forward CG position by allowing your orderly surroundings to bring you inner peace.

THE IMPORTANCE OF ACCOMPLISHMENT

The morale value of accomplishment cannot be overstated. Even in normal times, we derive a tremendous amount of fulfillment and pride from accomplishing things. How do you feel when you finish your to-do list? It's a great feeling when everything is going well and it's even greater when you really need a shot in the arm. The tasks themselves keep your mind focused and will give you an outlet for your energy. They allow you to express your creativity and provide a distraction from the crisis or emergency itself. If you find yourself sheltering in place, do not allow yourself to sit around bored, listless and afraid. Make a plan and accomplish things. It might save your sanity or even your life.

The pursuit of independent education can be one of the things you decide to accomplish. You can read up on something that interests you or something you really think you ought to know. Your knowledge base may come in handy and it definitely contributes to the strength of the whole group. Each capability, resource or subject familiarity a group member has makes the whole group a harder target and increases the chances of everyone's survival. So do some homework: Your knowledge project might just be the difference between boosted and disastrously low morale.

CONVERSATION AND KNOWLEDGE BASE

The oldest form of entertainment and relationship-building is conversation. If you find yourself in a survival situation with others, you will need to be a good talker and listener. If you have a talent for telling stories, you will be a hero. Preparing to contribute to a conversation requires two essential ingredients: a prior knowledge base and a healthy imagination. Read up on interesting things and be prepared to share what you learned—not in a way that makes you the teacher and the listener your student but in a way that feels like an interested person sharing things with interested people. If you can, keep a book of writing/story prompts or trivia, like *Guinness World Records*, as a conversation starter.

John Wayne and Margaret Lindsay in *The Spoilers* (1942).

Don't forget or neglect your active listening skills. Look the speaker in the eye. Try leaning forward as they speak or vocalizing your understanding of the content. Nod in agreement. Ignore distractions and give your undivided attention, summarizing what was said. Make the speaker feel like the most important person in the world to you while they talk. This facilitates good communication and conveys respect to the speaker, which is good for group unity and cohesiveness. Don't sell anyone short, either: as Ralph Waldo Emerson wrote, "[E]very man I meet is my superior in some way, and in that I learn from him."

EMOTIONAL LOWERING

ISASTERS, EMERGENCIES and crises are emotionally volatile and difficult. Emotional lowering begins when you recognize your heightened emotional state and decide to do something about it. You can go back to the basics of the fulcrum principle and see which of your three categories is weak and needs an investment. Lower the volume of your voice and slow your rate of speech. Try some box breathing by breathing in for four seconds, holding your breath for four seconds, breathing out for four seconds, holding your breath for four seconds and repeating the cycle. Tap your thumb and forefinger together and focus on the sensation. Take inventory of every input hitting each of your five senses and really notice each one. Remind yourself of your name, the date and your location. Smile. Sing. Be kind to yourself and others. There are many ways to emotionally lower yourself or someone else. This is valuable when someone is headed toward panic. It helps to reset and regain the ability to think instead of just feeling.

THE CIRCUIT-BREAKER

When you find yourself heading down into a dark thought spiral, there is a way to break that circuit and get your psychological feet under you again. Look left and notice what you see. Look right and notice what you see. Look straight ahead and notice what you see. Think a totally different and unconnected thought and say it out loud.

Richard Jaeckel, John Wayne, John Agar and Forrest Tucker in *Sands of Iwo Jima* (1949).

This could be anything from "That cloud looks like a lighthouse" to "Boy, I sure love ice cream sandwiches." As long as it's not related to your current troubles, it should work. This thought acts like a circuit breaker to your psyche when you are trapped in negative thoughts and emotions and helps give you some stability while you find your emotional balance again.

CONFLICT RESOLUTION

Nothing kills morale like conflict. The cohesiveness of your group may wind up being the only resource you have in a crisis, in which case you won't be able to go it alone—you'll have to work together to survive. Conflict resolution becomes a critical skill, and everyone will have to be on the same page and give it the same effort to make it work.

The best thing you can bring to the resolution of any conflict is a willingness to listen without judgment. Hear the opposition out and look for common ground. Maintain an attitude of respect and patience and be very aware of your body language, tone of voice and facial expressions. Make sure your whole body is conveying the same message. The only way to resolve conflict is through communication, so establishing and protecting this is foundational. Each person needs to feel heard, understood and valued in order to keep talking and listening.

Kindness goes a very long way. You're all facing a great deal of stress, no matter how long this emergency situation lasts. Establish rapport through your united message of valuing the person and legitimizing their fears or concerns. Find common ground and look for a solution that addresses each party's needs. Keep the lines of communication open and keep the group together. As the saying goes: a cord of three strands is not easily broken.

WHY MORALE MATTERS

Morale is the linchpin of every situation. No matter what stockpile you've accrued or what firearms you're proficient at using, morale can make or break the entire thing. People naturally feel they need to process negative inputs, so they linger on those thoughts and dwell on those emotions. This is a terrible habit.

When we dwell on or keep returning to a thought or feeling, we are laying down a new neural pathway in our brains. We are, in essence, teaching ourselves how to think and training ourselves to get comfortable in a particular homeostasis. Since we rarely feel we need to process positive inputs, we spend only a fraction of the time lingering there in our thoughts and feelings. That is why we create so many more negative neural pathways than positive ones.

If you want to change that paradigm, you can choose to cut positive grooves in your brain by intentionally holding on to positive thoughts, emotions and memories. If you're upset with someone in your group, this might look like remembering all the ways in which they've helped you or others, made you laugh, done kind things or otherwise been a good friend over the years. It might mean digging deep and feeling empathy for someone whom you'd rather not cut any slack. Doing this is a shock to the ego but it pays dividends in terms of establishing harmony and retraining your brain to look for the good. Granted, this is easier with some people than it is with others, especially if there's a history involved. But in an emergency, chances are whatever issue you may or may not have with each other is not nearly as important as ensuring you make it out alive. Little else needs to matter in the face of that objective.

Don't be hard on yourself if you find yourself struggling with this. Building new habits and neural pathways takes time, so be patient with yourself (and others) and know you'll reap the rewards of your hard work in due course. Be the bigger person and keep cutting those positive grooves every way you can.

MINDFULNESS

 HE ART of mindfulness is trendy at the moment, with everyone from yoga teachers to psychologists pitching their particular brand of presence and awareness. But the techniques involved in being a more mindful person are ancient. This discipline is essentially a way to cement yourself in reality and release all the thoughts that cause you to build tension and feel stress. There are many ways to achieve a mindful mindset, so try out a few exercises below and see what works for you. Like any meditative practice, you might not feel the effects right away, but build it into your daily life and you'll reap the benefits.

GET GROUNDED

Achieving a sense of being grounded is one of the chief reasons for practicing mindfulness. Ground your identity by asking yourself these questions: *What is my name? Who am I? Where did I come from? When was I born?* These questions ground the mind and renew a personal sense of identity in the midst of chaos and confusion. You can also ground your body by asking yourself the following questions: *What do I see? What do I hear? What do I feel (physically)? What do I smell? What do I taste?* Take your time and try to answer each question as comprehensively as possible. You can ground yourself to your surroundings by asking questions like: *What time is it? Where am I? What is today's date?* You can ground yourself to your emotions by asking yourself: *What do I feel? What provoked that feeling?* The important thing about grounding your feelings is to remember not to be judgmental, even with yourself. You can ascertain what you feel and why you feel it without insinuating that you shouldn't be feeling it. Feelings simply are. They exist and one is as valid as the other. Acknowledge the feelings you have without

John Wayne in
Operation Pacific
(1951).

judgment and then move on. Do not judge and do not
dwell. Let it come in, feel it, acknowledge that you feel
it, then let it go.

THE BODY SCAN

The point of this exercise is to focus on individual areas
of your body and gradually release tension in each until
you feel somewhat relaxed.

Sit in a chair or lie down in a comfortable position.
Starting at the crown of your head, feel the tension in
your forehead, eyebrows, eyelids and cheeks. Clench
and relax your jaw along with the rest of the muscles
in your head, pause a moment, then move on to
your neck, shoulders, arms and so on. Target every
muscle you can find and consciously relax it. As you're
doing this, allow your mind to go wherever it wants.
Acknowledge and accept whatever feelings arise.

THE FOUR-LEGGED FRIEND

This exercise is designed to allow you to acknowledge the emotion that wants to be acknowledged without handing it the reins. You can notice what you feel when you feel it and then gently send it back to rest.

Imagine your feelings are a friendly cat (you can also imagine a dog, if that's your preference) taking a nap in the sun. While your feelings are quiet and inactive, the cat sleeps soundly. When a feeling is triggered, the cat wakes up, looks around sleepily and stands up slowly, stretching. Then it walks lazily over and nuzzles your hand for attention. Imagine yourself petting the cat's head, then sending it back to take another nap in the sun. When another feeling is triggered, imagine the scene again, focusing on seeing how smoothly you can send it back to where it was snoozing without letting the thought or feeling affect your mood.

THE NATURE SCENE

If your shelter-in-place scenario permits you access to the outdoors, take it upon yourself to go outside and practice mindfulness in nature.

You can observe leaves falling in the breeze or gliding along a stream and imagine each one is a separate thought or feeling. Notice them, then watch them tumble to the ground or pass out of sight. If you're stuck inside, reflect on your favorite season or your favorite place to relax and incorporate that setting into your mindfulness practice. Find what works for you and stick to it.

HOW MINDFULNESS HELPS

Consider that by adopting mindfulness practices, you're holding yourself accountable for the places you allow your mind to go, the feelings and memories your brain mulls over in moments of strife as well as quiet pauses. If you struggle with maintaining a positive mindset or seeing the good in people or things, mindfulness can help you let go of negative emotions and recenter your focus on positive, happy or healthy things.

Mindfulness can teach us how not to judge ourselves, which we can then extend to others. If you can figure out what you feel and why you feel it, then normalize and legitimize the feelings for yourself, you can do it for others.

Box breathing—inhaling for four seconds, holding for four seconds, exhaling for four seconds then holding for another four seconds—lowers the heart rate and blood pressure and helps translate your sense of emotional well-being into a state of physiological well-being. (For more on this breathing exercise, see pg. 84.) Mindfulness encourages experiencing the present moment and not dwelling on the past or worrying about the future.

FOOD

YOU CAN'T be too picky about mealtime when you're sheltering in place. (To be honest, you'll most likely be glad to have something to eat, period.) But while this type of emergency scenario won't yield dishes you might see on a Michelin-starred menu, it also doesn't mean you have to eat nothing but cans of baked beans day after day. There's a happy medium and it doesn't have to break the bank. With the right preparation ahead of time, you can keep yourself not only fed but properly nourished. When stocking up before hunkering down, be sure to consider all of the food groups, just as you would when grocery shopping any other time. Variety will be kind to not only your stomach, but also your mind.

LONG SHELF LIFE OPTIONS

One of the primary concerns in a shelter-in-place situation is having enough food. It will be nice to have your pantry, cabinets, cellar, refrigerator and freezer present instead of stuffing a backpack full of food to evacuate. There are several different categories of food-based readiness. We will start with long shelf life options, which you can purchase early and organize in advance, leaving yourself minimal effort when an emergency situation arises.

These are going to be things like dry goods: rice, flour, sugar, dried beans, dried peas, dried lentils, potato flakes, dry grits, dry cream of wheat, dry oatmeal, powdered milk, powdered electrolytes, powdered eggs, 25-year freeze-dried survival meals, dried backpacking meals, powdered butter, muffin mix, dry pancake mix, dried noodles, baking powder, yeast, baking soda, salt, spices, cornmeal, powdered bullion, dried soups and more.

John Wayne
in *Red River*
(1948).

For canned goods, you'll want to stock canned fruits, canned vegetables, canned beans, canned coffee, canned meats, canned fish, canned milk, canned jellies, canned sauces and more.

As you amass your survival pantry, pay attention to shelf life and expiration dates. Eat from the front, replace to the back. That means to keep the oldest items in front and eat from those in normal times, buy replacements and put the new items in back to keep your stock rotating and as fresh as possible.

SPICES AND SEASONINGS
Nothing kills our ability to enjoy a well-cooked meal like bland flavor. Flavor inspires us to eat and makes us happy, increasing our morale.

SPICES TO KEEP ON HAND

- ☐ Brown sugar
- ☐ Bullion in all flavors
- ☐ Cayenne
- ☐ Celery salt
- ☐ Cinnamon
- ☐ Clove
- ☐ Curry
- ☐ Dried ginger
- ☐ Dry gravy mixes
- ☐ Dry soup mixes
- ☐ Garlic powder
- ☐ Italian seasoning
- ☐ Lemon pepper
- ☐ Nutmeg
- ☐ Onion flakes
- ☐ Onion powder
- ☐ Oregano
- ☐ Paprika
- ☐ Parsley flakes
- ☐ Pepper
- ☐ Saffron
- ☐ Sage
- ☐ Salt
- ☐ Sundried tomatoes
- ☐ Thyme
- ☐ Turmeric

Remember the principle of force multipliers. Stock spices that have many purposes and applications. Also be sure to choose complementary spices so you can experiment when you start to get bored. A few common combinations to start with are cinnamon/cayenne, turmeric/oregano and ginger/chili powder.

MORALE FOOD

Morale foods are all things you like to eat regardless of whether or not they're good for you. After all, looking after your mental health is important too, and ice cream (or bacon, or whatever you love) can be a big boost for mind. In fact, according to a study conducted in Finland, delicious, familiar food releases endorphins, creating a chemical change in our bodies that makes us happier.

Examples of morale food include chocolate, pretzels, popcorn, chips, candy, brownies, cake, pie, ice cream, cookies, danishes, muffins, pastries, fresh berries, fresh cream, scones or even classic comfort foods like macaroni and cheese, mashed potatoes, shepherd's pie, fish and chips, french fries, cheeseburgers, tacos, fried chicken or anything else you particularly love. The point isn't what the food is or how good it is for your body. The point is how good it is for your mood and how much you enjoy it. Have some things in your stock of provisions that will allow you to raise morale and reward you for having survived to this point. Don't forget comfort drinks like coffee, tea and hot cocoa.

CARBOHYDRATES

When it comes to stocking a pantry for long-term storage, the easiest category is carbohydrates. Pasta, rice, flour, dried or canned potatoes, prepackaged macaroni and cheese, Rice-A-Roni, frozen bread, canned biscuits and crescents, ramen, Cup Noodles and the like are the college student's—and the emergency-prepared person's—best friends. However, when the time comes to eat, don't get too reliant on carbs. They taste good and are very filling, so it's easy to carb load and forget about the other food groups. That leads to weight gain, loss of energy, fuzzy thinking and general malaise. By all means, stock up your pantry with carbs, but use them wisely. In a shelter-in-place situation, the carbs are the easiest and cheapest to stock and prepare. In a bug-out situation, however, they are the hardest category of food to obtain and prepare. So you'll want to pack your go bag with the easiest options available, and that usually means carbs in the "just add water" category such as pasta or freeze-dried, carb-heavy meals.

FREEZE-DRIED FOODS

Like any other type of food, you should stock what you enjoy eating, but you won't know what that is if you're not familiar with freeze-dried foods. Some favorite freeze-dried meal brands to try:

- AlpineAire
- Backpacker's Pantry
- Mountain House
- My Patriot Supply
- Peak Refuel
- Ready Hour
- Ready Wise
- Survival Frog

PROTEIN

Proteins are made up of chemical building blocks called amino acids that your body uses to build and repair muscles and bones and to make hormones and enzymes. They can also be used as an energy source. As such, protein will continue to be very important for your overall health and stamina in an emergency situation, but your usual sources might not be as abundant. So you'll have to plan ahead intelligently.

FRUITS AND VEGETABLES

Fruits and vegetables are the hardest to stockpile, but there are ways to do it. You may can your own foods if you grow them or buy them fresh. You can buy canned fruits and vegetables. You can find freeze-dried fruits

COMMON SOURCES OF PROTEIN WITH RELATIVELY LONG SHELF LIVES

- ☐ Artichokes
- ☐ Asparagus
- ☐ Beans
- ☐ Broccoli
- ☐ Brussels sprouts
- ☐ Buckwheat
- ☐ Canned fish
- ☐ Canned meat
- ☐ Cheese
- ☐ Corn
- ☐ Dried fish
- ☐ Freeze-dried meat
- ☐ Frozen fish
- ☐ Frozen meat
- ☐ Jerky
- ☐ Legumes
- ☐ Millet
- ☐ Nuts
- ☐ Oats
- ☐ Powdered eggs
- ☐ Powdered milk
- ☐ Protein bars
- ☐ Protein powder for milkshakes
- ☐ Quinoa
- ☐ Rice
- ☐ Soy products
- ☐ Teff
- ☐ Wheat

and veggies to a certain extent but they're not as plentiful as freeze-dried carbs and meat. Usually, they are mixed into a freeze-dried meal like fried rice with vegetables or mango with sticky rice. You can turn fruits into jams, jellies and preserves. You can dehydrate or candy fruits as well. You can buy bags of dried apricots, prunes, raisins and cranberries. Peas dry and rehydrate very nicely, as do tomatoes. You can buy banana, apple and coconut chips. Coconut milk or coconut water will give you some of the coconut's nutrients. Dried strawberry or banana granola or apple cinnamon oatmeal will work too.

FREEZING AND REFRIGERATION

If you have a basement or cellar, you already know that it's always cooler below ground. If you are able to make big blocks of ice (freezing 2-liter or 1-gallon bottles of water), you can convert your freezer in to an icebox. See pg. 100 for more on how to do it.

AT-HOME DEHYDRATING AND FREEZE-DRYING

There are plenty of options available to consumers for dehydrating your own food at home. This is certainly the most cost-effective option but it's also the most time-consuming. It also requires you to get familiar with spices and seasonings. When you reach for something you dried and packaged yourself, then rehydrate and cook it, it comes with a deep sense of satisfaction.

BOTTLING AND CANNING

If you have the time and inclination, it's possible to can your own fruits and vegetables, as well as make and bottle your own beer, mead, pickle juice, soda and many other things. There are several methodologies for both that can be found in online DIY forums and home-brew communities. What's important is to understand why these are valuable options. If you grow a garden, you have the option of putting some of that valuable produce away in case of an emergency. In a shelter-in-place scenario, fruits and vegetables will be your most difficult category of food to fill. When you grow your

KNOW YOUR BRANDS

While Harvest Right is THE name in at-home freeze-dryers, some of the top dehydrator brands include:
- Chefman
- Cosori
- Excalibur
- Gourmia
- GoWISE
- Nesco
- Presto

own, you can concentrate on the things you like and skip the things you don't. You can season produce according to your own taste. You know where it's been, from seedling to table. There are no chemicals or hormones in it unless you put them in. If you have a health or religious dietary restriction, you can set your own conditions. If you come upon hard times such as losing a job or weathering a disaster, you have already provided nutrition for yourself for the leaner times. You control the date and shelf life. You get maximum nutrition out of your produce. You save money when you don't have to buy store-bought goods. As a bonus beyond these facts, there's also a significant quality of taste difference between garden-grown canned fruit and store-bought canned fruit.

HOW TO BUILD A WALK-IN FREEZER

When you've got things that need to stay cool, you can't rely on electricity to do the job. Here's how to build your own refrigerated space at home with your own two hands.

First things first: Construct some sort of cover or use a garage, shed or other existing structure to get the job done. It just needs to be shaded.

You will need
- Sawdust
- Blocks of ice (1-foot cubes work best)

1. Put down a layer of sawdust on the floor, then lay the blocks of ice on top. You do not need to line the walls with the ice—you can build it as shown on the right.
2. Cover the blocks with 2 inches of sawdust and pack the dust in between the ice blocks as much as you can.
3. Add more ice blocks and more sawdust for a total of three or four layers.

NOTE: This space will not freeze food, but it will keep things chilled. Make sure direct sunlight is never shining on the sawdusted ice blocks or all your hard work will melt. The ice will last according to its size, so larger blocks will last far longer than 6-inch cubes. Over time, you will eventually need to replace the ice, but it can last for months in the right conditions.

GOODS that you want to keep chilled can be stored on shelves, as you would in a pantry. Keep these organized so you can grab what you need in a flash. No need to dally here and add your body heat to the room.

SAWDUST, when packed tightly, will work to insulate your ice and prevent air from getting to it, which will cause it to melt.

WATER

HETHER YOU'RE facing a major emergency or just going through your routine on an ordinary Wednesday, water is crucial to survival. Many of us are guilty of occasionally taking this resource for granted, though, which is why you can never be too prepared when it comes to securing as many sources of H_2O as possible prior to potential disaster. The place in which you're sheltering might seem well-prepared to provide plenty of water, but you still have to think about possible scenarios such as your

Sophia Loren and John Wayne in *Legend of the Lost* (1957).

sources running out or becoming undrinkable. With all of the other dangers you could be facing, you don't want to add the effects of dehydration to the list.

WATER SOURCES

Water sources will vary depending upon your location. While you might continue to have running water in your home for a time, be prepared for that to change. If you have a well, you are in good shape but you will need a generator to access the water. If you have a water source on your property, you will benefit from not having to haul it very far. If you don't, you may have to go hunting for a creek, stream, spring, fountain, well, river, pond, lake, dam or even a substantial puddle. You can construct a solar still (see pg. 106). If you are in a wooded area, look for low ground with thickening vegetation. That will lead you to water. If you have a map of any kind, water is always depicted in blue. Sometimes you have to really look for a thin blue line on the page because all that's there is a stream. You will not find surface water around porous rock. It will all soak in and gravity will draw it down and out of your reach. You will only find water in saturated areas or ground that is impermeable. Be prepared to filter, boil or purify the water you obtain from any natural source.

WATER STORAGE

Storing water is pretty straightforward, but there are some things you do need to know. If you have bottles of untreated, natural spring water, it will turn yellow and start growing things if left in place too long. It must be treated with some sort of stabilizer to be good for long storage. According to the Centers for Disease Control and Prevention, you can use regular, unscented chlorine bleach with 5-9 percent sodium hypochlorite to do this, but you only need a tiny bit. Add no more than 8 drops per gallon of water. Mix or shake it thoroughly throughout and let it sit for at least 30 minutes before drinking. If the water you're looking to purify is cloudy, you can add up to

WHAT TO STOCK TO STORE WATER

- ☐ 1-gallon water containers
- ☐ 5-gallon water containers
- ☐ 50-gallon water containers
- ☐ Chlorine bleach with 5-9% sodium hypochlorite
- ☐ Potassium permanganate
- ☐ Glass jars or metal pots for boiling
- ☐ Water filtration system
- ☐ Portable water filters
- ☐ Tools for digging
- ☐ Shaded area for storage

16 drops of bleach—you'll still have to wait at least 30 minutes before drinking. If you are going to let the water sit somewhere for long-term storage, add the bleach at the beginning. There are numerous containers you can choose from. It depends on where you want to keep it. You can fill empty 1-gallon milk jugs and 2-liter soda bottles with water. You can use a 5-gallon water jug, a 6-gallon mylar bag or even a 55-gallon drum. Make sure your containers have never held toxic chemicals, no matter how long it's been. Clean and rinse any potential containers thoroughly before filling them and treat them with bleach right away.

Store your containers of water in a cool dry place that has no chemicals around it, such as gasoline or pesticides. Certain containers can leach chemicals right through them and they will show up in your water. Fill the containers all the way to the brim before sealing them and do not allow air to be trapped inside. If you intend to purchase storable water, make sure it has been treated and is shelf stable.

WATER PURIFICATION

You can (and should) boil, filter or otherwise purify water. Sometimes, you may wind up doing some combination of the three. If you choose to boil it you will want to do so for 30 minutes in order to kill any bacteria. Start with twice as much as you want to use because steam will cause rapid evaporation. However, steam is pure and can be collected and used for drinking. You just need a water-impermeable slanted surface above the steam upon which it can condense and run down into another container of your choosing. This doesn't need to be boiled—you can drink it right away.

Chlorine, chlorine dioxide or iodine are the chemicals usually found in water purification tablets. Potassium permanganate can also be used to purify water. You can get these in loose crystal or tablet form from Amazon or stores like REI, Eastern Mountain Sports and Dick's Sporting Goods. Make sure to follow the directions carefully. It takes only the smallest amount to work and just a little too much can make you quite sick. A little more than too much can be fatal. Note that this will turn your water pink or purple. Mix it completely throughout the container and let it sit for 30 minutes before using it.

Filtering is another option and can be used in conjunction with boiling or purifying. Filtering simply catches the particulate matter in the water and screens it out. You can install a water filter on your kitchen faucet or in your refrigerator water dispenser or keep a pitcher with a filter on top in your refrigerator. You can also buy portable filters for camping and hiking or filters that attach to the mouth of a 5-gallon jug. You can even construct your own out of fabric and activated charcoal. You have options for making water safe but do not trust it right from the source. Waterborne bacteria can make you very sick and in some cases even kill you.

HOW TO MAKE A SOLAR STILL

Finding water can be a daunting feat and will require time and energy. Do not wait until you are dehydrated to get started on this. If you are without water rations, prioritize this immediately after constructing your shelter. If you can work on it after the sun goes down that will help conserve your body fluid. You will have to wait overnight for water to collect.

You will need
- A large, clear plastic tarp
- A place to dig
- Rocks (or other weighted objects)
- A clean container to catch the water

1. The larger your tarp, the more water it will collect, but you need to be able to seal all the edges to prevent evaporation. Dig a funnel-shaped pit. The opening should be just a little smaller than the surface of your tarp.
2. Place a collection cup, bowl, bag, etc. in the center of your pit.
3. Spread your tarp out to cover the hole entirely and seal the edges with dirt, sand, rock or any other weighted material you can scrounge. Place a weighted object like a rock in the middle of the tarp to create a funnel shape. This makes a path for the condensation to travel down into your collection point. Make sure the low spot in the tarp is aligned correctly and will drip right into your basin.
4. Go to sleep and check your basin for water in the morning. The deeper you dig, the more moist the sand or dirt will be and the more condensation it will produce.

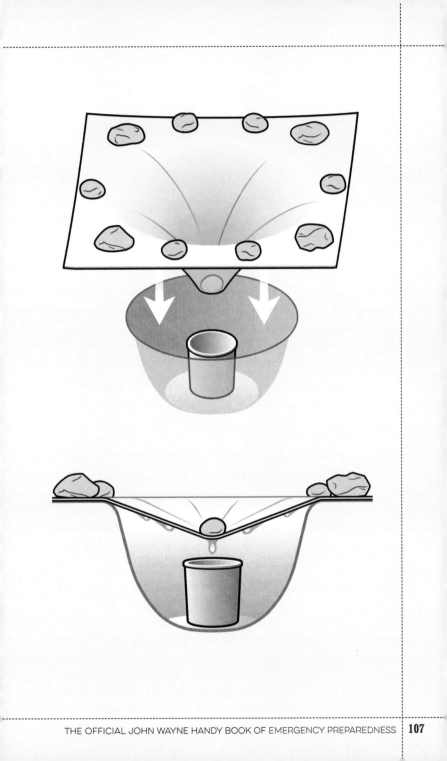

HOW TO MAKE A BUSH STILL

When you can't find an abundant source of water, it's time to get creative with plants. Learn how to collect water via condensation. It takes time (overnight) but can work when you're in a pinch.

You will need:
- Several clear plastic bags (as large as possible)
- Access to bushes and/or trees

1. Look for low-lying bushes and trees. If you see cattail reeds, jewelweed, palm fronds or any other type of water-reliant plant, you're in business. Willow trees, water maples and sycamores are all good choices, too. Make sure your chosen foliage has access to direct sunlight for at least part of the day.
2. Grab as much of the bush or as many branches of the tree as you can bundle together and envelop them in the clear plastic bag. Seal the branches inside by tying the bag closed.
3. Wait, typically overnight. Water in the soil will be drawn up into the branches and condense on the leaves. With the plastic around it, the condensation will have nowhere to go—gravity will cause it to drip and collect in the bottom of the bag.
4. Keep the bottom area of the bag (the water collection point) clean and clear of debris, since this will hold your drinking water. The more plastic bags you put out, the more water you'll collect.

DON'T RATION YOUR WATER

It may sound counterintuitive, but rationing water can land you in a world of trouble. If you find yourself in a situation where you have only a small amount of water on hand and have no idea when you'll be able to get more, drink what you have right up front. The actual good it does for your body now is of far greater value than the potential good it could do at some later point. People have died from dehydration with water still in their reserves because they deprived themselves of this critical life-sustaining resource. Don't let yourself make that mistake.

Of course, you'll need to determine how much water to stockpile in order to accommodate your household's needs. For storage planning purposes, a good rule of thumb is to stock enough for a consumption rate of one gallon per person per day. Keep enough on hand for two weeks at that rate. You may need even more if you are in a hot or dry climate or if you anticipate the possibility of becoming pregnant or ill. If you store tap water, replace it every six months and treat it with chlorine bleach with 5-9 percent sodium hypochlorite as described on pg. 103. If you store purchased water, keep it in the shade and as cool as you possibly can.

COOKING

NOW THAT you're all stocked up on food, you'll have to consider the ways in which you'll prepare it. If you're sheltering at home, you might still be fortunate enough to have access to amenities such as microwaves, gas or electric stoves and toaster ovens. But any of these convenient options can be taken away at any time in the event of an emergency, so it's best to have several backup plans in place. You may have to turn to more primitive methods than you're used to, which is why it's imperative that you familiarize yourself with other means of cooking and gather any supplies you'll need in case you have to get creative.

COOKING WITH AND WITHOUT GAS

If you have a gas range and a gas oven you will have more options for cooking even if the electricity goes out. That is not to say your fuel will continue uninterrupted—providers of gas rely on electricity to meter usage and most gas stoves, ovens and fireplaces use electricity to ignite the flame. You may have the option of lighting the flame manually with a match or lighter and then using it normally until you are done. Even if you have a backup generator for powering your home you might want to consider dropping in an underground gas tank to run it. If it is functioning properly, gas cooking should not emit a smell but your food still will. Keep in mind that wafting delicious aromas out the windows in a disaster situation may bring hungry people to your door. If you create smells that escape the house, be prepared to share your food or defend your home. You can mitigate this somewhat by keeping the windows and doors closed and sealed while

(continued on page 114)

John Wayne and George "Gabby" Hayes in *Blue Steel* (1934).

COOKING ESSENTIALS

- ☐ Aluminum foil
- ☐ Baking soda
- ☐ Cooking oil
- ☐ Fire retardant gloves
- ☐ Flour

- ☐ Knives
- ☐ Powdered butter or milk
- ☐ Powdered spices
- ☐ Skewers
- ☐ Tongs

HOW TO MAKE A TEEPEE FIRE

If you're ready to cook and no longer have a working stove, build a teepee fire. It doesn't retain its shape for long, but the initial channeling works well to get it started. You can maintain this fire for as long as you can feed it, so make sure you have extra firewood ready to go.

You will need
- A spark
- Tinder
- Kindling
- Logs

1. Pick a spot in a cleared area and lay your materials out around you.
2. Light your tinder on the ground. When it catches, begin to lay your sticks of kindling down. Once your kindling catches fire and burns reliably, take your logs and place them vertically around the base of the fire, leaning in toward the center and resting on each other at the top, teepee style.
3. As the fire burns, the logs will fall toward the center. This fire needs to be maintained and even reshaped from time to time. Eventually, you'll simply find yourself laying fresh logs straight down on the fire to keep it going. It will not look like a teepee in the end, but the initial shape did its job up front by allowing a high volume of airflow.

cooking to contain as much of the smell as you can. If you enjoy a lot of spices (such as cumin, rosemary or turmeric) in your meals, those smells will travel farther faster and linger longer after the cooking is done. You can cook on gas-powered grills outside but there is no way to contain or mask the smell of your food cooking. If you must do your cooking outside but aren't in a position to share, post a person or two on watch duty to give you early warning if your handiwork is drawing attention so you can move back inside and secure the house if necessary.

COOKING WITH AND WITHOUT ELECTRICITY

If the power goes out and all you have is an electric range and oven, you will need to come up with a backup plan. As always, a generator is useful. You may want to also consider an outdoor grill or smoker. You can get them in gas-powered or charcoal/wood-fueled varieties. If you have a fireplace, you have another option for cooking. Consider investing in an old-fashioned stovetop tea kettle. You can cook many things if you can boil water. One option is to have lots of dehydrated and freeze-dried food that only requires boiling water and time to reconstitute to cook. You should be able to rig something to use your kettle over a fireplace, brick oven, outdoor fire pit or grill. Electric stoves, ovens, kettles and griddles are a fine option if your electricity is on or if you have a generator that will power them. They are smokeless and odorless and can help you maintain an image of having no more than everyone else around you.

CAMP STOVES

There are many options and types of camp stoves available. Jetboil is an option that uses a propane fuel canister attached to a thermos-like device for boiling water. BioLite makes a unique stove option that burns just about anything flammable you can scrounge, has attachments for grates and griddles and produces electricity while it burns. Coleman makes a gas option too. Just do a little research to see which style you like. There are grills, ranges, griddles, kettles, thermoses and more. All have unique and valuable applications and can be used for hiking and camping trips as well as emergency preparedness. Be aware that the gas-powered options were not designed to be used indoors due to the fumes they can produce. The wood/charcoal burning options are likewise meant to be used outdoors since they can be a fire hazard. Take your time to read up on the options and only buy what makes sense and you are willing to use. Always use new gear once or twice in normal conditions to ensure you know everything about it before you really need it.

CAMP STOVE SAFETY TIPS

- Never light a stove of any kind and leave it unattended. Make sure the area is clear of anything that can catch fire unintentionally.
- Choose a spot out from under low-hanging tree limbs or branches. Have a 5-gallon bucket of water at hand for dousing a runaway flame.
- Do not light a camp stove indoors. Be aware of gas fumes and make sure your area is well ventilated. Watch for signs of a headache and shut the gas off if one develops.
- Choose or make a spot with a natural fire break like a body of water or a patch of dirt immediately downwind.

GRILLING

You can grill just about anything: beef, pork, chicken, fish, lamb, bison, vegetables, etc. You can even make things like eggs if you have a frying pan or some aluminum foil. You can bake flour-based things like muffins, breads and cakes by wrapping the dough in foil or placing it into a Dutch oven and then directly nesting it down into the hot coals. You can boil water in a saucepan or a tea kettle or even an individual tin can or cup, just be careful about handling them. Use oven mitts or grill gloves to avoid melting other materials or getting burns. You can make a meat course, starch, vegetables, hot drinks and dessert all on one grill. It can truly turn your backyard into a kitchen.

BOILING

It's good to have options in both ways to generate enough heat to boil water as well as vessels in which to boil it, as this is a capability you cannot afford to lose. The ability to boil water will be the most important aspect of emergency food preparation (to say nothing of your medical, hygiene, and water purification capabilities—you can even melt wax crayons and other spare bits of wax together to make a candle if you have the ability to boil). If you stock up on canned vegetables, freeze-dried and dehydrated foods and certain types of meats, all you really have to be able to do to make them edible is boil water. You can do this in an electric tea kettle, on the stove, in the oven, in the fireplace, over a fire pit, on the grill or over a camp stove. If you have the ability to regulate water's temperature for a significant period of time (either with a sous vide circulator or a

POTLESS HOT POT

You can cook a simple, filling meal with whatever protein, vegetables and spices you have on hand, whether that means a beef, spam or squirrel dinner.

1. Put your meat, vegetables and spices together and wrap them in foil.
2. Place the foil pack directly onto the hot coals and leave it alone until cooked. Usually about an hour if you start with raw meat.

NOTE: The smell will not be controlled. It will go wherever the fire's smoke blows, so be prepared for company.

working stove) you can expand your repertoire to include cooking eggs, fish and a host of other delicate foods in hot water. You can make coffee, tea, hot cocoa, hot cider, wassail and other drinks too. Your menu will be at its most comprehensive when you have the ability to boil.

ROASTING AND SMOKING

If you want people to wander over, roast something. Roasting may produce the most sumptuous meats but it also produces the most tempting smells. That said, it is a good way to prepare large cuts of meat or whole animals. Plus, if you're roasting a piece of meat that large, chances are you'll be fine with sharing it anyway, so roast away, but do so intelligently. Smokers use low levels of indirect heat to cook over the course of 8 to 24 hours and infuse the food with a smoky flavor. Smoking is another method that creates amazing smells, but instead of smelling the meat itself, smoking produces a woodsmoke aroma. Both methods produce wonderful smells and can attract attention. Both take time and require careful attention. They are better for outdoor cooking than indoor cooking, although you can roast your meat and potatoes in the oven too. Roasting also usually requires several hours and uses direct heat, so make sure you have the proper amount of time and space.

HEATING

FTEN IN emergency situations, we can't rely on our usual methods of staying warm. You might have to think outside the box if your electricity fails and the temperature drops. The good news is you don't necessarily need your HVAC certification to stay toasty in a pinch. There are plenty of ways you can stay prepared, from the obvious—like a fireplace—to the more intricate, like a terra-cotta pot heater. And if you're stranded outside, you can always use the fire-building skills on pg. 112.

FIREPLACE

Having a fireplace is an incredible asset in a shelter-in-place situation. A fireplace is good for heating, cooking, drying, lighting, sterilizing, maintaining morale and a whole lot more. It draws people to it, helps people bond, and makes them more comfortable. Fireplaces do provide good heat but usually only to the room they're in. Unless you have multiple fireplaces, you cannot expect to heat an entire house with this method. In a survival situation, one warm room is generally all you need. Make sure to have enough cut and dried firewood to last for a season. That gives you time to figure out a new plan or to get more.

CLOTHING

Clothing is your first level of shelter and your last line of defense against cold. If you find yourself in a shelter-in-place situation in cold weather, start by dressing warmly. If you wear warm pants and socks, a shirt plus a sweater and a jacket or coat and have a sleeping bag, you may not even miss the ambient warmth of a heated house. While you can put your sleeping bag in front of the fireplace for the night, the clothing you choose can allow you to forgo the fire and still be plenty warm and comfortable all night long. If you are not allergic to lanolin, wool is a great choice. It provides

John Wayne in
Island in the Sky
(1953).

HOW TO RECOGNIZE HYPOTHERMIA AND FROSTBITE

Hypothermia is simply losing heat faster than your body can replace it. You might be surprised to know it can happen on a hot day as well as a cold one. Shivering is the first sign of hypothermia as the body fights to generate more heat to keep up with the rate of loss. The time to intervene is when you first begin to shiver. You can preempt the rest of the problem by dealing with it right then (as opposed to waiting to see if it will resolve itself—it won't).

The effects of this early stage can be reversed through active heating: taking a hot shower, changing into dry clothes, eating and drinking hot things, wrapping up in blankets, sitting close to the fire, cuddling up with a heated blanket, using a heating pad or hot water bottle, getting out of the wind, etc. Your body will naturally protect your core the longest, so your job will be to protect your extremities. Cover your hands, feet and face and take every measure you can to prevent frostbite.

If frostbite does occur, do not choose active warming measures as you did for hypothermia. Instead, choose passive warming, like getting out of the cold, tucking the affected area under arms or in between legs. Do not rub the skin or use hot water to get warm. Do not thaw any tissue that might refreeze. Drink warm liquids to warm yourself from the inside out (but steer clear of alcohol for now). As your skin rewarms, you might feel a tingling or burning sensation. Take over-the-counter pain relievers as needed and seek medical attention for moderate to severe frostbite.

warmth whether it is wet or dry, wicks moisture away and acts as a natural deodorizer. There are also modern synthetic fabrics that do the same things. Dress in layers so you can make small adjustments to your temperature whether you want to warm up or cool down. Use as few layers as possible while you are working hard and then add more when you stop and cool down. Don't allow yourself to stay covered in sweat once you cool down. That will put you behind the power curve for warming back up and can start you on the road to hypothermia. Sheltering in place is especially beneficial to making necessary changes in your clothing, as you can continue to live out of your closet and, if you still have water and electricity, do laundry as usual.

BLANKETS

In advance of encountering a shelter-in-place situation, ensure you have a range of blanket sizes and materials for a broad temperature spectrum. You will want something oversized and very heavy like a bedspread, down comforter or sleeping bag for comfort while you sleep. You might want a few smaller wool blankets for portability and to leverage the amazing properties of wool. Sheets and towels definitely improve quality of life and also have many uses beyond bedding and bathing such as wound packing, medical bandages and dressings, rappel harnesses, privacy screens, litters, temporary walls, gear coverings, temporary pillows, awnings and more.

SPACE HEATERS

Space heaters usually conjure up the image of an electric fan-looking contraption with red, heated coils. While old-school space heaters will get the job done as long as you have power, they aren't the only option. A fireplace is technically a space heater in that it does not heat far beyond the space it actually occupies. Wood- or pellet-burning stoves are another good non-electric option for heating a space. Steam from cooking and boiling will heat a space but does so with high levels of humidity. In a cold environment, this can be a boon since cold air can be so dry. Chemical-based heat packs for hands and feet are a type of space heater, as are hot water bottles, electric blankets and heating pads. If you get to keep your electricity, you get to keep all your options. If not, you get to be creative.

COOLING

IN CASES of extreme heat, temperature regulation is critical. From simple shade to the most high-tech portable air-conditioning units, it's best to have several redundant options in case one fails. Nothing is too simple: stay indoors if possible, keep some microfiber cooling towels in your bag or if you're more of a gadget-fiend, invest in an air-conditioned shirt—yup, they're real!

FREEZER
Cooling is a bigger challenge than heating. If your shelter-in-place situation happens during the summer in a hot climate, your challenge is going to be finding ways to keep cool. Your freezer is a very good first option since it functions like a cooler and can stay cold for a while even after losing its power source as long as it stays closed. That is why it is a good idea to take the time now to freeze some 2-liter bottles of water and place them throughout and between your frozen foods. Keep a generous amount of ice made for the same reason. The thicker each individual piece of ice the more it can resist the warming air. A fully stocked freezer will stay cold longer than a partially empty one.

REFRIGERATOR
We've already discussed how to make an ad hoc refrigerator. If you lose electricity, use that knowledge and prioritize consuming everything that has the potential to develop harmful bacteria like salmonella. Drink the milk. Eat the eggs, meats, fish, yogurt and cheese first. Then go back and eat the fruits and vegetables. There are some things that will last a long time, like condiments and juices. You can transfer a couple of frozen 2-liter bottles to the refrigerator to extend its useful life as well. Pack the foods with the

John Wayne and Alex Havier in *Back to Bataan* (1945).

lowest heat tolerance in between or underneath them. If you have a medication in your life that requires refrigeration, you need to come up with a way of ensuring the continuity of your cooling system. Aside from the ways we have already addressed, if you have fresh running water on your property you can immerse sealed packages of perishables in it. The water will act as a refrigerator. However, if you retrieve it and the water has leaked into the container, do not risk ingesting it. It might make you sick. If the weather is cold, you can put things outside. If your refrigerator is running on electricity from your generator, make sure to create gaps and channels between and around your food. Refrigerators cool by circulating cold air and packing your refrigerator full will prevent it from fully cooling.

HOW TO RECOGNIZE HYPERTHERMIA AND HEATSTROKE

The number one culprit of all heat injuries is dehydration. First and foremost, ensure your level of hydration is and remains adequate. If you have work or chores to do, take however many breaks you need to take in order to get the water your body requires.

Everyone gets warm from exertion, but an early warning sign of a heat injury is nausea. If you're in a hot climate or generating your own heat from exertion and you start to feel nauseated, stop what you're doing and take a break. Get out of direct sunlight and hydrate. Rest, shade and hydration can prevent a heat injury. If that doesn't reverse it, use active cooling measures like cold water and moving air. Wet your clothes and body, especially at the neck, armpits and groin and fan yourself. Evaporative cooling is very efficient and only requires water and moving air to generate if the day is dry. If the day is wet and rainy, evaporative cooling will not work. In this case, wet your clothes and body and lie still. Unless you have a fever, your body temperature will come down.

If you or someone in your party has a particularly high body temperature or throbbing headache; feels confused; is slurring their speech; has hot, dry skin; stops sweating despite the heat; or begins to have seizures or loses consciousness, these are all signs of heatstroke, which can be fatal. Seek medical attention immediately. Young children, elderly individuals and people with certain health conditions are more susceptible to heatstroke, so keep an eye on them and don't assume their symptoms will improve with time.

WATER-BASED COOLING

As previously stated, fresh running water like a stream or river can cool food, so it can also bring your body temperature down, too. Water from a garden hose, a well or even a swimming pool will do nicely unless it is very shallow and has been sitting in the summer sun for a long time. You can shower or bathe in cool water to beat the heat, or you can even take a sponge bath. The human body lowers its internal temperature by using evaporation. That's why we sweat. The evaporation of water off our skin allows us to cool down more rapidly, which is why it's hard to feel comfortable on very humid days. Seek shade and use it. Prioritize adding ice, an ice pack or a wet cloth to your head, the back of your neck, armpits and groin. You lose most of your body heat through your head, so keep that in mind and use it to your advantage. Your neck, armpits and groin are the intersections of your major arterial highways and can quickly circulate cooled blood to the rest of the body. Using water to aid evaporative cooling, moving air (a breeze or a fan) and shade together is going to be your best bet for beating the heat.

CELLAR
The temperature below ground is relatively constant: between 50 and 60 degrees Fahrenheit. That is why your basement or cellar feels so good in the summer. Seek these spaces for cooling.

You can take it a little further by laying down and stretching out directly on the cool ground. Caves and caverns can be quite chilly when they go below ground due to the natural below-ground temperature, constant shade and air currents. This is why, before the advent of electricity, folks kept perishables fresh in root cellars naturally cooled by the earth. If you have access to any underground space, keep it in mind as an alternative for cooling.

John Wayne in
The Searchers
(1956).

BUGGING OUT

SOMETIMES YOUR BEST BET FOR SURVIVAL IS TO LEAVE THE COMFORTS OF HOME AND HEAD OFF THE GRID.

MEDICAL SUPPLIES

N EVERY survival situation, there's a hierarchy of needs and priorities that can help you stay calm and focused when your brain is obsessing over a cascade of data points to consider. Your most important need—the first thing on your priority list—is ensuring you have access to life-saving medical intervention should you or someone in your household require it.

Most people pack as if food is the first priority. You can live for weeks without food but only days without water and only hours exposed to harsh elements or with a life-threatening injury or illness. Your second priority will be finding or building shelter, because whether the climate is hot or cold, protection against the elements is a must. Only once those needs have been met can you move on to the third item: the follow-up treatment of life-threatening issues and lesser problems.

Perhaps someone has sustained a break, a burn or an allergic reaction during the process. If they had any kind of need for an immediate medical response earlier on, they will now need to circle back and re-check their work and perhaps do more than they could when they were on the move and still in danger. For those keeping score at home: Your next priority will be building and maintaining fire for warmth, cooking, hygiene, sanitization and morale, then finding and purifying or filtering water. Your last priority is finding food.

Once you decide it's time to bug out, you open yourself up to a whole new range of data points to consider before making your next move. Now that you're no longer sheltering in place, you need to start

John Wayne and Beulah Bondi in *Back to Bataan* (1945).

ITEMS TO CONSIDER ACQUIRING
FOR A BUG-OUT SCENARIO INCLUDE
BUT ARE NOT LIMITED TO:

- ☐ 850 paracord
- ☐ Ammo
- ☐ AR pistol
- ☐ Base layer
- ☐ Batteries
- ☐ Blousing bands
- ☐ Book
- ☐ Bowls
- ☐ Cams and wedges
- ☐ Carabiners
- ☐ Cargo pants
- ☐ Compass
- ☐ Deck of cards
- ☐ Dehydrated food packs
- ☐ Deodorant
- ☐ Down blanket
- ☐ Eating utensil(s)
- ☐ Emergency medical kit
- ☐ Energy bars
- ☐ Figure 8 descender
- ☐ Fishing line and hooks
- ☐ Flashlight
- ☐ Flint
- ☐ Folding shovel
- ☐ Fuel
- ☐ Hammock
- ☐ Hand crank flashlight
- ☐ Hand crank radio
- ☐ Handgun
- ☐ Harness
- ☐ Hat for sun
- ☐ Hat for warmth
- ☐ Hiking boots
- ☐ Kettle
- ☐ Knife sharpener
- ☐ Knives (fixed blade and folding)

thinking in terms of deciding what to take and what to leave behind. A good rule of thumb is to only pack what you can carry by yourself for several miles over rough terrain, which means space and weight are at a premium. Look for essentials that are durable enough to withstand the elements but light enough that you don't throw your back out when you transport them. This basic but effective criterion will narrow your choices of what to bring and, if you're being honest

- ☐ Leather gloves
- ☐ Leatherman multi-tool
- ☐ Lighters
- ☐ Lip balm
- ☐ Lock picks
- ☐ Matches
- ☐ Money
- ☐ Mylar blanket and tent
- ☐ Passport
- ☐ Pencil sharpener
- ☐ Pencils
- ☐ Rappelling rope
- ☐ Rescue 8
- ☐ Shirts
- ☐ Solar charger
- ☐ Solar-powered lantern
- ☐ Stove
- ☐ Straps
- ☐ Sunblock
- ☐ Sunglasses
- ☐ T-shirts
- ☐ Tactical tomahawk
- ☐ Toilet paper
- ☐ Toothbrush
- ☐ Toothpaste
- ☐ Towel
- ☐ Trail soap
- ☐ Tubular nylon webbing
- ☐ Ultralight 850 down jacket
- ☐ Underwear
- ☐ Wallet/ID
- ☐ Water
- ☐ Water bags/bladder
- ☐ Water filter
- ☐ Water purification tablets
- ☐ Waterproof paper
- ☐ Wool socks
- ☐ Ziploc bags

with yourself, how much you're capable of carrying. For example, instead of lugging around your unwieldy arsenal of a tool kit, perhaps one trusty, pocket-size multi-tool would suffice. Instead of bringing a full complement of fishing gear and tackle, perhaps a couple of fishing and cordage cards would do the trick. Sure, you might think it's counterintuitive to head out someplace where you have no idea what you'll encounter, where you're less prepared than you are at home, a familiar place where you've evaluated the risks and know your needs to a fault. But bugging out means embracing the risks, trusting that anything you find could turn out better than the scenarios you'll face while stuck at home. What matters most is that you can lift and carry your gear. You should also consider that if you're able to head out in your vehicle, great—you can take that much more with you. But if you have to leave on foot, you'll be quite limited, so don't drive yourself crazy trying to fit your supplies into every available square inch.

FIRST AID KIT

If you have not yet taken a wilderness first aid course, now is the time to sign up. This is the ideal way to learn how to stabilize and treat illness and injuries in the field, where you are far from a hospital or any kind of formal medical care. You'll even learn how to package and evacuate patients. A must-have for an adventure of unknown proportions is a well-stocked first aid kit. Plan on bringing everything you need to stop or control bleeding of any magnitude: tourniquets, Israeli dressings, hemostatic gauze, hemostatic dressings, roller gauze and chest seals.

Susan Hayward and John Wayne in *The Fighting Seabees* (1944).

CLEANLINESS

They say it's next to godliness for a reason, and when you're wounded, keeping clean becomes even more important.
Infection is your greatest enemy in the wild. After an injury, you should first use water to flush wounds but ensure the water has been boiled, filtered or treated beforehand. You can sterilize metal instruments by placing them directly into an open flame for 30 seconds. The fire will blacken the metal. Wipe it clean and use it for removing splinters or ticks, lancing boils and even making sutures.

Take it from the experts: Non-stick burn pads and burn gel are the only humane way to treat burns in the field. You'll also want to counter potential breathing difficulties with a supply of nasopharyngeal airway tubes. Topical antiseptic is a must. You can combine a couple of SAM Splints and a handful of triangular bandages to create splints and slings (for more on splints, see pg. 62). Emergency mylar blankets help prevent hypothermia and shock. Moleskin works well for blister treatment. Duct tape—which trumps gravity as the one force holding this world together—can be used for bad cuts, field expedient tourniquets and many other things. Wrap open wounds with sterile dressings and medical tape. Treat traction splints with paracord and carabiners. Benadryl does wonders for mild allergic reactions. Depending on your allergies or existing conditions (more on that below), Advil, Aleve, Motrin and Tylenol are effective when it comes to handling pain, and aspirin is key in a heart attack situation. Since all of these are lightweight and you'll have no way of knowing what you might encounter, pack all you have.

MANAGING PAIN WITHOUT MEDS
Biofeedback is the practice most people turn to for lowering pain and anxiety without medication. It can be done by a medical professional and incorporate special technology or you can practice the principles on your own. The categories of biofeedback are breathing, heart rate variability (HRV), muscle tension, temperature, skin conductance, blood pressure and brain waves. You can use box breathing (see pg. 91) to accomplish a great deal. This lowers anxiety, heart rate and blood pressure together. You can scan your whole body and consciously relax your tense muscles one group at a time, or you can cool your body temperature by sitting still in the shade. You will not be able to

THE THINGS YOU MAY ENCOUNTER IN A BUG-OUT SITUATION COULD INCLUDE MEDICAL ITEMS AND MEDICATIONS TO TREAT THE FOLLOWING:

- Allergic reactions
- Bites
- Blisters
- Breaks
- Burns
- Chills
- Choking

  NOTE: Choking is something you may encounter as your makeshift sustenance situation evolves, but like near-drowning, this one requires knowledge and skill rather than a piece of gear to solve. Become familiar with the Heimlich maneuver and, if possible, take a CPR class to make sure your last meal isn't what kills you.

- Cuts
- Dehydration
- Diarrhea
- Fever
- Frostbite
- Heart attack
- Hyperglycemia
- Hyperthermia
- Hypoglycemia
- Hypothermia

- Infections
- Gunshot wounds and piercing/impalement

  NOTE: You might need hemostatic gauze and dressings, a pressure (Israeli) dressing, one or more tourniquets and possibly chest seals depending on the location of the entry and exit wounds. Familiarize yourself with these products beforehand so you don't have to learn on the fly while someone is in danger.

- Nausea
- Near-drowning
- Shock
- Sprains
- Stabs
- Stings
- Traumatic amputation

  NOTE: Hopefully, this won't be something you ever have to consider, but just in case, stock medical-grade roller gauze, a pressure dressing, a tourniquet and a mylar blanket to treat shock.

- Trench foot
- Vomiting

change or manipulate every category without training and equipment but you can impact these basic aspects.

LIKELY HAZARDS

Part of caring for the people in your household involves factoring their known medical conditions into your planning. As far as likely hazards go, a known issue is at the top of the list. This could be diabetes, a late-term pregnancy, a broken wrist or any other health consideration. Plan and pack with one eye on the issue. It sounds like a lot at first glance, but remember that you can disperse the medical gear

across multiple people's packs. As long as the group has what it needs, your first aid doesn't have to be carried by one person. And if you're traveling alone, you can rule out every medical issue you know you don't have and limit your supply to accommodate your needs and risk factors.

COMMON WOUNDS
AND HOW TO TREAT THEM

By following the simple tips provided, you can buy yourself time and start on the road to recovery.

1. Blisters, scrapes, cuts, bruises and sprains/strains are the five most common outdoor wounds. Keep a blister kit like moleskin, nylon knee-highs, duct tape or skin glue to both cover the blister and act as a friction absorber to prevent them from worsening. You can stack the deck in your favor by wearing nylon knee-highs as a base layer under socks. When you do this, the friction will rub between the nylon and the sock instead of being between your skin and the sock.
2. Scrapes and minor cuts do not need to be closed but must be kept clean to avoid infection. Irrigate the open wound with clean water. Pat it dry. Add a topical antibiotic like bacitracin to act as a prophylactic and cover it with a clean dressing. Wounds should be checked and dressings changed twice a day in the wild.
3. Bruises and sprains need to be treated symptomatically. Take pain medication with an anti-inflammatory for comfort. Splint the area if needed.

MORALE AND BOREDOM

MORALE AND boredom can be just as big a problem in a bug-out situation as they are in a shelter-in-place situation. Between the moment you know you need to leave and the second you've set up camp, boredom won't even be on your radar—you'll have plenty of work to do. But as soon as the wood is chopped; the fire is blazing; your fish, deer, turkey or other meat is roasting over a crackling fire; and you're taking a moment to consider how you've come this far, it creeps up on you. You might just eat and go to sleep utterly exhausted, but when you wake up in the morning and can't decide what you should do because your usual routine no longer exists, you'll need to control your inner dialogue and have your shields up. Now is the time for positive self-talk, optimism and hope. Seize the day by assigning yourself tasks and accomplishing them. Inventory your belongings and make breakfast. Exercise. Engage in the practices of your faith and pray. Focus on what's possible and what you have already accomplished. Remember: You're far better off than before you left home, and that counts for something.

PLAYING CARDS

As we mentioned on pg. 76, playing cards are versatile while sheltering in place, but they're even more valuable in an emergency situation. Playing cards make for an excellent choice when it comes to packable entertainment. They contain an untold number of possible games, whether you use them alone or play with others. Small and lightweight, a good deck of cards entertains the brain and boosts morale by preventing boredom and inspiring healthy

John Wayne and Ward Bond in *Tall in the Saddle* (1944).

competition. It's the multi-tool of the game world. You can even get waterproof or washable decks that are sure to last. Grim Workshop even makes a deck of cards that feature a different survival tip on each card. The late great James Rowe was a U.S. Army Green Beret who was captured by the North Vietnamese and spent more than five years in captivity as a prisoner of war. He slowly but surely constructed a deck of cards for himself out of pieces of paper and cardboard to defeat the tedium resulting from being caged like an animal. He was so successful he went on to found the U.S. military's SERE (Survival, Evasion, Resistance and Escape) training program. No one could ever convince him a simple deck of playing cards was not enough to make it through such a harrowing experience.

John Wayne in
Hondo (1953).

BEYOND A STIFF UPPER LIP

Here are a few ways you can improve your own attitude as well as those of others who look to you for guidance during times of struggle.

- Name 10 things, people or places for which you are grateful.
- Smile.
- See how many times a day you can thank others.
- Take a walk and pick out 10 things that look beautiful or smell wonderful.
- Choose to be humble when you have the opportunity to brag.
- Help others.
- Serve someone.
- Look for ways to make a positive difference to your situation.
- Find ways to win by looking for the small victories in everything.

A GOOD ATTITUDE
Your attitude will make or break your whole situation. In fact, lack of practice or experience in the field can be overcome with ingenuity, imagination, a willingness to try new things, a can-do attitude and an optimistic outlook.

On pg. 88, we outline how mindfulness strategies can be useful while sheltering in place. These same techniques could be the difference between merely surviving and thriving in an emergency. Optimism and positive thought patterns will spill over onto the people around you and inspire them to follow your example. When you arise as the natural leader it will be because your attitude is so compelling in the way you look out for others, take necessary risks, do the hard work yourself, hear people out, never complain, figure things out, tackle challenges and motivate your group to believe they actually can do this successfully. No one wants to be around complainers who revel in pity parties rather than put in the necessary effort for success. Those are alienating traits, while inspiring fulfillment, purpose, focus, determination, strength and humility are traits that will draw people to your side. If you treat all others with respect and grace, they will be loyal to you and look out for your well-being.

RESISTANCE BANDS
Resistance bands look like enormous colorful flattened rubber bands. They usually come in a pack of five, each a different color and strength. You can use these to replace weights for building muscles. When stacked and folded, they are not much bigger than a deck of cards and very light; however, if used properly, they can replace an entire weight bench. You can use them to build new muscles, restore injured joints to strength, rebuild atrophied muscles and even train combative skills. You can use them solo or for team-

(continued on page 144)

THREE SIMPLE RESISTANCE BAND EXERCISES

Work the muscles you'll need most as you keep in shape for or during an emergency.

1. ROTATOR CURLS

Stand with your feet shoulder width apart and hold the resistance band as shown. Keep your right arm flexed and stationary while pulling the band with your left hand toward your left shoulder, rotating your shoulder in the socket as you pull your left hand back. Perform 10 reps, then switch hands so that your left arm is stationary as you pull with your right. Do 10 more reps and perform three sets on each side.

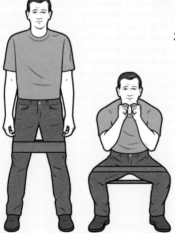

2. RESISTANCE SQUAT

Place the band around both legs at mid-thigh. Stand with your feet shoulder-width apart and squat down, keeping enough tension in the band that it stays around your thighs for the entire movement, then slowly stand back up. Begin with three sets of 10 and work your way up over time. When it becomes easy, increase the number of sets, the number of repetitions and/or the strength of the resistance band.

3. STANDING LEG ABDUCTION

Place the band around your legs at the calf. Place your weight on one leg and anchor it down as you lift the opposite leg away from the standing leg and out to the side, against the resistance. Begin with three sets of 10 and work your way up over time. Switch legs and repeat. When it becomes easy, increase the number of sets, the number of repetitions and/or the strength of the resistance band.

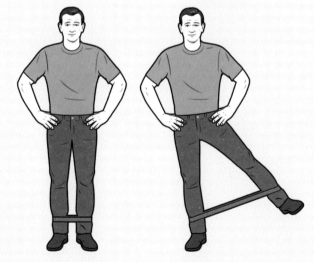

A NOTE ON GETTING THE MOST OUT OF YOUR TOOLS

Quality tools will seriously enhance your capabilities in the field. It isn't a stretch to say your life may depend on your choice of tools and your ability to use them. In order to rely on them, they must be made by manufacturers you trust. They've also got to be the right tool for the right job—you can't count on every product out there to be a multi-tool if it isn't labeled as such, otherwise you could risk injuring yourself or others. In other words, don't use a tool in a way for which it was not designed, i.e., don't use your pliers as a hammer. It might be tempting if you're on a tight budget, but don't skimp on quality. If you must make a sacrifice, give up quantity before quality. Look after your initial investment by conducting routine maintenance. Use a Scotch-Brite scrubber to scrub off any rust or salt that collects on the surfaces. Keep your tools clean and oiled. Tighten the screws as needed. Use protective coverings like leather sheaths or canvas bags to prevent impact damage and minimize scratches. Respect the tools and handle them with care. Try to avoid overly rough handling like throwing them, dropping them or running over them if possible.

building exercises. You can mount them to a tree and expand your options for isolating muscle groups by 100 percent. You can even use them as lashings for shelter, weapons or rafts or as springs for traps and snares. Small and lightweight, they are a must have.

MULTI-TOOLS
Leatherman, Swiss Army and Gerber are the names that spring to mind when the word multi-tool is spoken, but multi-tool can refer to any multi-purpose force multiplier—duct tape is a great example. It can mend and repair clothing and shelter, waterproof packs, help to heal cuts, stabilize fractures, replace tourniquets and do as many things as we can imagine. Card decks do this by supplying an enormous array of

games. Grim Workshop makes knives, axes, adzes and all manner of survival tools no bigger than a credit card that can each do dozens of things. They are small, light and designed to fit in a pocket, in a wallet or on a belt. These micro-treasures can make a huge difference to your quality of life when you are in the wilderness trying to make or construct something and wishing you had some tools to help you. Paracord is another great example of a true multi-tool. There aren't enough pages in this book to list out all its possible uses, so always keep some with you. It can help you erect a shelter, make a harness or string a stretcher. TOUGH-GRID is an amazing and durable paracord available in several different strengths. Potassium permanganate (which you can find at most outdoor sporting goods stores) can start fires, purify water, treat wounds and infections and clean and preserve produce. Activated charcoal can filter water, draw toxins out of wounds and absorb poison. When you pack for bugging out, choose the items that have multiple uses to maximize your use of space and weight. Ask yourself: Is this item a multi-tool? And don't forget to use your imagination.

RECOMMENDED MULTI-TOOLS

☐ Leatherman Rebar

☐ Leatherman Sidekick

☐ Leatherman Wave

☐ Victorinox Swiss Tool MXBS

☐ Victorinox Swiss Tool Spirit XBS

FOOD

 UR BODIES require fuel to keep functioning, plain and simple. When we're at home, we have all the comforts of ensuring our nutritional needs are met, not to mention we're usually an arm's length away from all our favorite cooking ingredients.

But things can look pretty different if circumstances dictate that you flee your humble abode in search of greener (read: safer) pastures off the grid. You're going to want to make sure you have food on hand that doesn't perish after a couple of hours unrefrigerated. Don't think you need to choose between what's tasty and what keeps, either—plenty of brands have managed to bridge this gap with ease, some of which you might even eat on a given workday or during a weekend hike. Here's how to make the most of that ever-present need to eat when you're far from the comforts of your kitchen.

COMMERCIAL OPTIONS
You can buy many different brands of ready-to-eat trail food ranging from jerky to dessert to full meals to individual ingredients. You might even decide you want to have a smattering of everything on hand so as to not tire of one item or flavor too soon. Before you stock anything, decide whether or not you'd be comfortable eating the same thing for a protracted period of time. If you have a choice in the matter now, act on it.

If you only pack full meals and you just need a quick bite of energy, you are more likely to forego essential nutrients because of the hassle involved. Having jerky, trail mix, trail bars, nuts, seeds, chocolates, dried fruit, fruit chips or some other option as a stopgap measure is a good idea.

RECOMMENDED BRANDS

JERKY

- Country Archer
- Jack Links
- Kirkland Signature
- Oberto
- People's Choice
- Tillamook

DRIED FRUITS & DESSERTS

- AlpineAire
- Backpacker's Pantry
- Clif
- Mountain House
- Peak Refuel
- Ready Hour
- ReadyWise

- Rind
- Solely
- Trailtopia
- Tru Fru

FULL MEALS

- AlpineAire
- Backpacker's Pantry
- Good To-Go
- Mountain House
- Nomad Nutrition
- Patagonia
- Peak Refuel
- Ready Hour
- ReadyWise
- Trailtopia

This list is far from exhaustive, but if you have no experience selecting jerky beyond grabbing what sounds delicious, it should give you a good start.

Of course, you're not limited to what your local outdoor sporting goods supplier has on hand. You can also go to the grocery store and buy Ocean Spray bags of dried fruits, Hershey's candy bars and Nature Valley trail mix and energy bars.

The secret to these foods' longevity on the shelf is their high sugar or salt content. Make sure you balance your salt intake against your water intake and your sugar intake against your exercise output when relying on these types of foods for sustenance. Keep your health and fitness in mind at all times—your survival hinges on them.

HOMEMADE OPTIONS

While your bug-out location might not have everything you need, you can make an "oven" of sorts to carry with you as you walk. If you buy or make a mylar envelope padded with bubble wrap you can use it to seal in heat and help you cook meals while you remain on the move. You can decide what you want to eat and pack the dried or dehydrated ingredients in a Ziploc bag. Double bag it for spill-proofing. Stop to boil water and add the boiling water to your dry ingredients. Seal both Ziploc bags and drop the closed product into the padded mylar envelope. Seal the envelope and put it back in your pack as you continue on. In roughly half an hour, your meal will be ready to eat.

You can also wrap your meat, vegetables, spices, butter and sauce or gravy in tinfoil. Double or triple wrap it for structural integrity. When you have a nice hot fire blazing, tuck the foil-wrapped meal down into the embers and let it cook. Depending on what ingredients you chose and how big the meal is, it will be ready in about 20-60 minutes.

You can dehydrate, freeze dry and vacuum seal your meals and pack them to take with you. Again, you will need to allow time for boiling water to reconstitute them.

You can make your own trail mix or trail bars out of your homegrown or fresh ingredients such as oats, wheat, millet, barley, whey, chocolate, coconut, raisins, dried cranberries, dried apricots, prunes, honey, banana chips, apple chips, cinnamon and whatever other ingredients you prefer for easy and quick energy, storing your snacks in air-tight containers, vacuum-sealed bags or zipper-lock bags. Though zipper-lock bags aren't quite as good as vacuum-sealed bags in terms of keeping things fresh, they have the benefit of being resealable if you break one open for a quick snack. You can carry coffee, tea, electrolytes, lemonade, Tang or other drinks in powder form for flavor and caffeine options as you go, similarly packaged.

OPTIONS FOR STORING
FOOD IN THE WILD

If you're going to store food somewhere off of your property, your number one concern will be protecting it so it's still there whenever you're ready to eat. Your best bet for this is to use man-made coolers with locking mechanisms that wild animals can't open.

But if you don't have that option, you can put the food in a dry bag or two to minimize the smell and string it up in a tree, high above the ability of most animals to reach. You can also put it into dry bags or sealed containers and sink it underwater in a pond, lake, stream, river, etc. You will have to weigh it down with something heavy enough to overcome the buoyancy of any trapped air. You'll also need to plan to include a retrieval system, like a line you can pull from the surface to bring it back up. This works especially well when your food needs to be kept cool, as the water will be far cooler than the air. You can dig a hole and place your food into it and cover it with a stone too heavy for the local wildlife to move. If you choose this option, be sure to dig your hole deep. Curious critters will try to dig to reach it if they smell it.

In all cases, the best practice is to use a sealed container or two or three dry bags to contain the smell. If you can successfully accomplish that, the battle is half won. Animals will not try to access something they don't realize is there. Industrial grade garbage bags are great for keeping things dry and containing smells as long as they are not torn. If this is the route you plan to take, place the food inside one bag and tie the opening completely closed. Place the filled bag upside down in a second bag, then seal the opening with a knot and/or a gooseneck. Place that bag upside down into a third bag and seal the opening the same way. Now you have three layers of smell containment and your food is back to being right side up. All that's left is to dig in.

WATER

 CCESS TO clean water is a must during any survival situation. Just as we don't cease needing to fill our bodies with food during an emergency, we still require hydration to stay alive and keep functioning. After all, three or more days without water will prove fatal, no matter how extensively you've crafted a survival plan. Here's how to keep the odds stacked in your favor by downing enough of that good ol' H_2O.

John Wayne as Ethan Edwards in *The Searchers* (1956).

CARRYING CONTAINERS

Water can be carried in a bottle, a canteen or even a bag. Bags are great for lightweight packability, but there's always a risk of it losing its usefulness due to a hole or a slice in the plastic.

If you do choose bags, carry several and protect them. Do not crease, cut or puncture them. Keep them out of direct sunlight. Don't let them dry out and crack but do not allow them to stay wet and grow mold or mildew either. The best way to ensure their lifespan is to fill them with shelf-stable water and keep them clean. Transport them full and continuously use them. Treat the water to kill bacteria and keep it from growing anything new.

Canteens and bottles are great for being robust and somewhat puncture-proof but have to be cleaned and maintained just like every other water container for your health and safety. There are some brands of filters that are designed to work directly with specific water bottles. You can carry water in hollowed-out gourds and in old-fashioned wooden buckets too. Use your imagination. The vessel simply needs to be impermeable. Even a plastic shopping bag, waxed canvas or a raincoat will work for a short duration.

PORTABLE WATER PURIFIERS AND FILTERS

There are numerous options out there these days for trailside water purifiers and filters. They each work differently and some cost more than others. They come in different shapes and sizes. No matter what you choose, be sure to try it before you truly need it so you know how (and if) it works. All the expenditure in the world won't save you if you don't have the knowledge to go with your purchases.

RECOMMENDED BRANDS

- Berkey
- Katadyn
- LifeStraw
- MSR
- Patriot Pure
- Sawyer

CHLORINE BLEACH

In a bug-out situation, you are probably not going to be storing water for an extended amount of time. You will probably draw it out of the source and purify or filter it every few days. That said, chlorine bleach does work to purify the water you are about to drink. The ratio is only 4 drops of bleach to 1 quart of water or ¼ teaspoon to 1.75 gallons. Make sure you shake or mix it thoroughly to ensure the bleach permeates throughout all the water. Let it sit for at least 30 minutes before trying it. Before you drink it, loosen the lid of your container, turn it upside down and allow the water to flush through the cap and mouthpiece to kill any lingering bacteria there. You should not be able to taste any bleach.

POTASSIUM PERMANGANATE

You can buy a jar of loose potassium permanganate crystals—which have several survival uses—but beware of the risks. It is easy to overdo it on water purification and drop too many crystals into the water. You can make yourself sick by overdosing and, if carried to an extreme, potassium permanganate can be fatal. The normal ratio is 3-4 crystals per liter of water. That is a ratio of roughly 1:10,000 parts. The powder itself is dark purple and a very few drops should turn your water pink. If the water turns darker pink or changes to purple the ratio is too strong. Throw it away and start again rather than risk getting sick. You can also buy potassium permanganate in tablet form.

WATER PURIFYING TABLETS

While you can use liquid bleach or potassium permanganate crystals, you can also buy tablets that are pre-measured and ready to use. There are a variety of brands, ingredients and countries of origin. Make sure to read the ingredients if you have any allergies so your survival situation doesn't go from bad to worse.

RECOMMENDED BRANDS

- Aquatabs
- Coghlan's
- Ef-Chlor
- Micropur
- P&G
- Polar Pure
- Potable Aqua
- Taharmayim

CLAY VESSEL FILTRATION

If you have a clay vessel to fill with filtering material (sand, gravel, rocks, grasses, charcoal, etc.) and it only has one opening, layer the material in the reverse order of the way you would if it was open at both ends. Place grass in the bottom, then layer on sand, gravel, pebbles and rocks. Pour the water in and give it time to get all the way to the bottom. Carefully tip the container over to pour the water back out. It will have gone backward and forward through the filtration system by the time it comes back out. If the clay is hard, you can also place it in the embers of your fire and boil the water inside as an alternate method.

John Wayne and
Paul Fix in *Back
to Bataan* (1945).

PLASTIC IN A PINCH

Heating plastic can release carcinogens and the vessel can melt if it
gets too hot. There's no visible way to tell the water's been affected,
which is why it's best to use glass or metal as a vessel for boiling
water. Should you find yourself in a situation where boiling water in
plastic is your only way to get what you need, suspend the plastic
above the fire and ensure it can stay at least 2–3 feet above the
flames. Try to save yourself the trouble by steering clear of plastic.

BOILING

There are several ways to boil water in the great outdoors, but all of them require fire. If you don't have a saucepan or teapot on hand, you can:

- Fill a glass bottle and place it in the embers of a fire to boil.
- Suspend your water container over the fire.

However you do it, if you're using it to make your water drinkable, let it boil for 30 minutes before drinking. Since boiling water evaporates into steam so quickly, start with twice as much water as you want to drink. You can also collect the steam by letting it condense on something—a pot lid, for instance—and drink that, too. Whatever object you use to collect the steam can be made of metal, glass or plastic. Don't use wood, though, since it will absorb the droplets.

When you boil water for drinking, do it twice: Drink one batch on the spot, then save the other for the next time you get thirsty so you'll have something ready to drink.

You can do the same with melting snow. If you are in a snowy environment, melt snow one batch ahead of the need so you always have ready-to-drink water. Boiling it to kill off any bacteria is the prudent thing to do—never let your thirst cloud your judgment.

HOW TO MAKE A FIELD EXPEDIENT WATER FILTER

Don't expect an abundance of safe drinking water wherever you go. Assembling an on-the-go water filter will help solve that problem and give you peace of mind.

Materials
- Activated Charcoal
- Clean T-Shirt or Sock
- Grass
- Gravel
- Knife
- Plastic Water Bottle
- Sand
- Small Rocks

1. Using a knife, cut the bottom off of a plastic water bottle. Keep the cap on and turn the bottle upside down so that the neck is pointing toward the ground. Stuff a piece of a (clean) T-shirt or a sock into the neck.
2. Pour some activated charcoal on top of the fabric, followed by a layer of sand, then gravel and small rocks. Finish with a layer of grass.
3. Cover the opening with another piece of sock or T-shirt.
4. Loosen the cap (which should be pointing toward the ground) and slowly pour water through the material over the opening you created, hitting the grass first and working its way down to the charcoal and out the other side. Large particulate matter will be filtered out first, followed by smaller matter, microscopic matter and then bacteria. If you can boil the water, do so.
5. Drink up!

NOTE: If possible, you'll want to wash the t-shirt after every use.

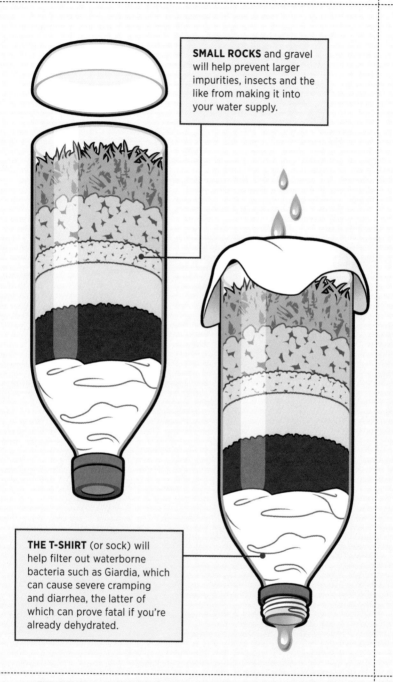

SMALL ROCKS and gravel will help prevent larger impurities, insects and the like from making it into your water supply.

THE T-SHIRT (or sock) will help filter out waterborne bacteria such as Giardia, which can cause severe cramping and diarrhea, the latter of which can prove fatal if you're already dehydrated.

COOKING

NCE YOU'VE secured shelter and water, you'll likely want something to eat besides trail mix (even though there's certainly nothing wrong with that). Variety is the spice of life, and if you decide to hunt or already have meat or vegetables on hand, you're going to want to know how to make it the tastiest meal you can.

John Wayne and Syd Saylor in *Born to the West* (1937).

COMMERCIAL CAMP STOVES

Commercially made camp stoves are wonderful devices engineered for outdoor cooking. They might do things differently by brand and type, but they all do it well. One of the considerations in a survival situation is how long your type of fuel will hold out. If you are dependent on propane canisters or hexamine fuel tablets, you will eventually run out no matter how many you have. An old-fashioned wood-burning camp cook stove like an Überleben Stöker Flatpack Stove, an Emberlit Stainless Steel Stove or a Unigear Wood Burning Camp Stove is an excellent idea to have on hand for a backup. These stoves are pre-manufactured but require a couple of minutes to set up. The nice thing about having one is that they burn wood, so your supply of fuel is nearly endless in wooded or forested areas. If you are in a jungle, rainforest, desert or vast snow-covered area, the propane or fuel cell options may be your best bet. BioLite stoves can burn wood, pellets, pine cones, leaves, pine needles, lint, clothing or any other combustible material. You simply have to keep feeding the fire and it will keep cooking your food. If you are going to use a propane or hexamine stove it is best to boil water and use the water to reconstitute dried foods. This is the most economical and efficient way to stretch your fuel out as long as possible. If you are going to rely on the heat of the fire to do the actual cooking it is far better to buy or build a wood-burning stove.

BOILING

The good news is you can boil almost anything to cook it, including meats, vegetables, grains, beans, roots and more. You will want to build an actual fire to accomplish this, and you can make a tripod for a pot or a kettle by following the instructions on pg. 160 or you can use a commercially available product, like a Qvien tripod. Once you have your tripod made you can suspend a pot, kettle or bottle above the fire to bring water to a boil. You can also set a non-meltable container down into the embers of the fire

(continued on page 162)

HOW TO MAKE A TRIPOD

Materials
- Three wet or green sticks of nearly equal height and strength
- Lashings/rope
- Non-meltable water container

1. Set the sticks up in a triangle roughly 2 feet apart from each other.
2. To bring the top ends together with lashing, knot a clove hitch on the first stick: Take the free-running end of the rope and place it over top the hitching line. Run it completely around, underneath to the left and over top to the right. It should form a Y. Bring the free-running end over top of the hitching line and up through the center of the Y. Pull it tight, then do the same with the second and third sticks.
3. Loop the rope around the three sticks six times, keeping the rope tight, then loop the rope between the first two sticks, followed by the second two sticks. Everything should be lashed tightly together.
4. Tie a knot around one end of your water container, then secure it to where you've lashed the tripod together, knotting it again.
5. Build a fire tall enough to reach the container, light it up and add water to the water container to start boiling.

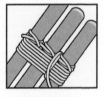

THE KEY to assembling an effective tripod is to ensure your rope is long enough so that the flames hit your water container and allow the water to boil. Hang it too high and you won't get the job done.

BE SURE to have extra firewood on hand that's dry and easily catches fire so your flames don't die out before the boiling is done. Depending on what you need the water for, this could go on for a while.

or construct a platform over the fire upon which to rest it. However you do it make sure your containment device will not melt or catch fire but can still get close enough to the heat to actually make the water boil. The ability to boil water is a non-negotiable necessity.

ROASTING

Roasting is your easiest way of cooking in the wild and requires no pots, pans, kettles or utensils. You can roast meat, vegetables and roots. If you do not intend to travel with a commercially-made roasting spit, you can construct one by following the steps on pg. 164.

HEAT PACKS

Chemical heat packs can be used to heat food if you have something into which you can seal them—just don't let the chemicals come into direct contact with your food.

If possible, enclose your food in plastic like a Ziploc bag and leave the heat pack on the outside. Military MREs (Meals Ready to Eat) employ this method of food preparation. You can buy MRE heat packs separately from MRE meals. This method requires you have some water and two layers of impermeable material. Your food needs to be sealed in one and that pack should be dropped into a second outer layer.

Place the heat pack into the outer chamber and add a small amount of water, which is the catalyst for the chemical reaction that releases the heat. Wait 10 minutes, then eat. It's that simple. This method does not cook food but it will heat pre-prepared food effectively.

STEAM COOKING

If you figure out a way to cook something unconventionally, you have a way to cook. Any port in a storm is a very accurate expression here. Be careful of using chemicals, such as Wetfire cubes or hexamine, and be very aware of keeping good ventilation no matter how you choose to cook.

A Swedish stove provides a heat source and a surface for cooking.

The recommended alternative to using chemicals is to construct a Swedish stove. This begins with a large log which gets split lengthwise into wedges. Reassemble the log upright with channels for air in between the pieces. If you have chicken wire, a wire clothes hanger or any other kind of non-flammable fastening material, you can wrap it around the base of the stove to keep the whole thing together.

FLAMELESS COOKING TOOLS

- ☐ GSI Bugaboo Base Camper Cookset
- ☐ GSI Stainless Troop Cook Set
- ☐ Lodge Dutch Oven Combo Cooker
- ☐ MSR Pika Teapot
- ☐ Sea to Summit Alpha 2.2

Place your tinder and kindling on top of the flat, top surface and light them. As they catch fire and begin to burn, let them fall through the cracks.

The shape of the "stove" will channel the heat directly upward and you can set your pot, pan, foil, etc. on top to cook food.

HOW TO MAKE A SPIT

Materials
- Six stout and wet or green sticks of similar length
- Lashings
- A long stick (to roast the food on)
- A knife

1. On one side of your fire, push three sticks into the ground in a triangle shape roughly 2 feet apart and tilt them toward each other until they make a tripod.
2. Lash them together as described on pg. 160, leaving the top of the tripod above the lashings available to mount the spit. Make another identical set directly across from the first set on the opposite side of the fire.
3. Using a knife, strip the bark off the stick for your spit and smooth it down.
4. Thread your meat or other roastable food onto the spit and lay the two ends of the spit into the V-shaped tops of the tripods. Your food should be suspended directly over your fire.
   NOTE: The more wet or green and flexible your tripods and spit are the less likely they are to crack, break or catch on fire.
5. Roast away...then bon appétit!

REGARDLESS of whether you like your meat or fish served rare at a restaurant or not, err on the side of caution and only eat food that's been cooked to well done to minimize the risk of food poisoning.

COOKED FISH flakes easily and is opaque. To check its doneness, take a fork and gently twist a small portion of the flesh. If it's translucent or resists flaking, keep cooking—don't take it off the spit yet.

UNLESS you enjoy eating thoroughly charred meats or vegetables, you'll want to turn the spit frequently to ensure the food is cooked evenly on all sides and the flames don't hit any one spot for too long.

HEATING

N A BUG-OUT situation, it's best to have redundancy in your stock whenever possible. When it comes to keeping warm, that means having multiple ways to start a fire, as well as several space blankets. These ultra-light blankets are great at conducting heat and can even be made into an impromptu shelter. Bear in mind that lighting a fire could easily attract unwanted attention.

John Wayne and Jean Arthur in *A Lady Takes a Chance* (1943).

FIRE

Fire building is an art. You have options for placement, what to burn, how to burn it and where to direct the heat. First, choose a place close enough to your shelter to keep you warm but not in a place where you run any risk of starting an uncontrolled fire. Look up as well as around to make sure you have enough clearing to maintain a controlled fire. If you can find or make a large stone wall, a cave wall, a brick wall or a mylar wall, you can build your fire a few feet in front of it. The wall will reflect the heat in the opposite direction.

Never build a fire inside a cave. This can cause rapid heating and expansion of the ceiling, leading to possible falling rocks. Do not heat river rocks. The rapid heating of stones that were cold a minute ago can cause them to explode, sending shrapnel in all directions. If possible, build your shelter about 5 feet in front of your fire on the opposite side of the reflecting wall for maximum heating efficiency.

Once you've chosen your location, you're ready to build your fire. Wood that is green or wet will not burn well. It will take a very long time to catch, if it catches at all, and will smoke and steam to an attention-getting extent. Look for dead and very dry wood. Fire requires three things: oxygen, ignition and fuel. The air itself will provide your oxygen source if you create your fire in a well-ventilated space and build in channels for the air to circulate through continuously. Your spark can be a match, a lighter, flint or even friction. Fuel is whatever you intend to burn. When gathering wood you will want to bring in three categories of burnable material: tinder, kindling and fuel. Tinder is an extremely fine material like sawdust or wood shavings. It is what catches the spark and turns it into flame just long enough to catch the kindling on fire. Tinder can be a bird's nest, dried pine needles, dryer lint, magnesium shavings, wood shavings or a chemical option like WetFire cubes. Some people like Vaseline-soaked cotton balls. Some people use sawdust mixed with oil or tallow. In any case, this is only the first stepping stone on your way to a blazing fire. The tinder ignites the kindling (twigs, small branches, etc.) and the kindling in turn ignites the logs. Your kindling should be no wider than a pencil: This is not what you will be burning all night, it's a bridge between the tinder that caught the spark and ignited the flame, to the logs that will keep you warm for hours.

CLOTHING AND BLANKETS

As we've discussed, plenty of items can be used in unorthodox ways when certain needs arise. Even your clothes can be a force multiplier if you plan ahead.

For items that can function as both clothing and blankets, military ponchos and poncho liners (affectionately referred to as woobies) do the trick. There is a Helikon-Tex product called the Swagman Roll: A poncho liner that converts into a sleeping bag. You can even cut holes for your head and arms in a large trash bag and put that on to trap your body heat. You can line your clothes with mylar emergency blankets or, in a pinch, newspapers to do the same.

To always be prepared, it's best to dress in layers in order to have the ability to make micro-temperature adjustments. Choose wicking fabrics in loose sizes. Do not wear cotton against the skin. It stays wet, does not wick and leads to feeling chilled. Keep your head and hands covered. Change your socks often, and always change them as soon as they get wet. Change out of wet clothes immediately. Strip down to one layer to do hard work and then put the other layers back on when you stop generating sweat. Wear rugged shoes or boots featuring waterproof material like Gortex with a Vibram sole.

Build a nest of bedding from blankets, pillows and sleeping bags for maximum comfort and warmth. Carry and use mylar emergency blankets to augment your warmth. Choose a sleeping bag appropriate to the overnight temperature spectrum in your area. You may need a sleeping bag that can handle sub-zero temperatures or you might live in a place where that would be a uselessly bulky item because the lows never get anywhere near that zone.

CHEMICAL HEAT PACKS

Chemical heat packs come in a range of sizes and are sold in pairs for the hands and feet. These items can mean the difference between keeping your digits or losing them to frostbite, so be sure to stock up.

CLOTHES FOR LAYERING

- ☐ Nylon knee highs or sock liners for a base layer under the socks
- ☐ Jacket with separable liner and shell
- ☐ Neck gaiter
- ☐ Leg gaiters

You can put heat packs in your gloves and shoes to keep your extremities warm while you walk or work. The chemicals are not kind to jewelry, though, so keep that in mind if you wear rings or a watch. They are capable of causing burns, but that scenario is extremely rare. You can get larger packs to slip inside your shirt or coat that function somewhat like a heating pad. You can even get sticky capsicum patches that use hot peppers to generate heat. The nice thing about these is that they stick where you put them so you are not constantly fighting to keep them where you want them. Do not use them on your hands and feet. They are for your torso, arms or legs.

CLOTHING BY ENVIRONMENT

IN THE MOUNTAINS, temperatures fall about 1 degree Fahrenheit with every 300 feet of altitude. Protect your skin and eyes. Minimize loss of fluids. Wear layers. Wear a head covering. Use eye protection. Have gloves on or with you. Wear a long-sleeved shirt. Wear long pants. Keep a jacket with you. Keep your feet dry.

IN THE ARCTIC TUNDRA, temperatures can be as low as -58 degrees Fahrenheit or -50 degrees Celsius. Protect your skin and eyes from windburn and snow blindness. Minimize loss of fluids. Wear layers: wicking, thermal and waterproof. Wear a thermal head covering. Use eye protection. Keep your head, face, body, arms, legs, hands and feet covered. Keep your body and feet dry. Use the acronym C.O.L.D.: Clean, avoid Overheating, Loose layers and Dry.

IN THE DESERT, the temperature spectrum between day and night can range from 30-130 degrees Fahrenheit or 0-50 degrees Celsius. Protect your skin and eyes from burns and glare. Minimize loss of fluids. Wear loose-fitting, light-colored layers. Wear a headscarf. Use eye protection. Keep your face covered to minimize inhalation of dust and sand. Keep your arms and legs covered. Wrap a piece of material around your neck for sunblock and wicking sweat. Blouse your pant legs or wrap legs in strips of cloth (gaiters) to keep sand out of your boots. Keep your feet dry.

IN THE JUNGLE, the temperature averages 50-80 degrees Fahrenheit or 10-25 degrees Celsius with 90 percent humidity. Protect your skin from bites, stings and punctures. Maximize evaporative cooling. Wear layers of light, wicking, quick-dry fabric. Wear wide-brimmed headgear to protect against dropping insects and snakes. Use eye protection against branches and vines. Wear quick-drying boots with drain holes. Keep your arms and legs covered. Carry a poncho for multiple uses. Blouse your pant legs or wrap your legs in strips of cloth (gaiters) to keep bugs out of boots. Keep your feet dry in breathable footwear and change your socks often.

IN AN URBAN SETTING, temperatures will vary by destination and season. Wear layers for maximum flexibility and utility. Wear clothing with plenty of pockets so you can easily carry everything you need. Match the styles of the local baseline. Wear comfortable shoes for walking and running. Do not wear restrictive clothing. Wear or carry a hat and glasses/sunglasses, should you need to switch up your appearance. Wear or carry a jacket.

IN WATERFRONT SETTINGS, the temperature spectrum is somewhere between tropical and freezing, depending on latitude and time of year. Protect your skin and eyes from burns and glare. Minimize loss of fluids. Wear loose-fitting, light-colored layers. Wear a head covering. Use eye protection. Keep your face covered to minimize sunburn. Keep your arms and legs covered. Wrap a piece of material around your neck for sunblock and wicking sweat.

MYLAR

As you've probably guessed by now, these lightweight, inexpensive blankets are an incredible multi-tool. You can line your clothes with them to seal in your body heat. You can make a wall out of them and use them to reflect the heat of your fire. You can use them to carry water or wrap cooked meat for travel. You can package a patient for evacuation. You can use them to treat shock. You can use them as a ground-to-air signaling device or to mark your trail for someone to find you. You can buy them in packs of 10 or 12 and stash them everywhere. They come in different sizes and strengths. They are even available in two colors, copper and silver, so you have options for signaling according to what shows up better in a given environment. They are so small and light they won't get in your way and offer a plethora of ways to save your life (or someone else's).

OTHER MATERIALS FOR STAYING WARM

In the woods, leaves and/or dry pine needles work well as insulators. In civilization, newspapers are a good substitute. Be sure to crumple up handfuls of newspaper and stuff many under your clothes. Bear in mind that it's not the paper that insulates but the trapped air. Your body heat will warm air trapped against you and create a barrier between you and the outside temperature. The more crumples there are, the more air gets trapped.

Anything that works to trap air will help keep you warm. To that end, you can use packing peanuts and other packaging materials, straw, dry grasses and more. You can also use a plastic garbage bag by cutting holes for the head and arms and wearing it like a poncho. Be aware that you want to avoid sweating as much as you're able, as this triggers evaporative cooling—the very thing you don't want happening right now.

A TEMPERATURE MULTITOOL

Extremity warmers come in several different varieties, from the 8-hour single use, shake-up pouches beloved by winter golfers and football coaches alike to some seriously more advanced tech. Keeping a few of those handy single-use warmers on hand can never hurt, but we prefer to also keep at least one of the following kinds of extremity warmers around. Having your fingers warm, nimble and ready to do fine motor work will dramatically increase your chances of being able to successfully cope with spur of the moment problems. If you can't grip your self-defense items because of the cold, you're in a bad way.

For decades, Zippo has made an easy-to-use, refillable hand warmer that's been a mainstay in hunting packs all over the country. You simply fill the chamber with Zippo fluid, light the wick, and cover the mini-candle with the top half of the device. Place that bad boy in a felt bag (Zippo provides one but a Crown Royal bag works just as well) and you're guaranteed to be warm and dexterous all day. Plus, you'll use less plastic waste than with single use warmers. These are best used in outerwear with a "Kangaroo" style single pocket on the front, which allows you to warm both hands at the same time.

Finally, in recent years, USB-chargeable electric hand warmers have also become popular. Zippo also makes these, as do a number of other companies specializing in outdoor goods. These are especially handy to have around, because when fully charged, they can also serve as a phone charger, giving you enough juice to get a call out to the outside world. These tend to be the most expensive, and increase in price with quality of battery life and secondary charging ability. This isn't the time for false economy: make sure you get something with as long a battery life as possible so you don't run out of warmth before rescue arrives, and make sure it's made with high enough quality materials that it can withstand the rigors of an emergency.

COOLING

 N SOME ways, keeping warm can be easier than fighting off the heat of the sun. It's easy to carry another layer or make a fire. Escaping the relentless sun can be a much more complex problem. Shade and hydration are the two aspects of cooling that are easiest to control, so make sure you have several light blankets to create temporary shade as well as a wide-brim hat and several liters of cold water.

ICE

When it comes to cooling, ice is worth its weight in gold. But for obvious reasons, it's difficult to rely on a steady supply of it when you're exposed to the heat. Ice is going to be the fastest way to cool down. Placing ice against the neck, armpits and groin cools the body the most rapidly and should be done in a hyperthermic situation like the onset of heat cramps, heat exhaustion and heatstroke. If you have access to ice, do not try to save it. The best thing to do is to use it while you have it. Do not hold the ice directly against the skin. Put a barrier of cloth between skin and ice to protect against frostbite. If you are treating a different medical concern like a burn of any kind, remove the ice for 10 minutes out of every 30 minutes to prevent the affected tissues from freezing.

SHADE

Shade is crucial in survival, as exposure to the elements will eventually lead to dehydration, hyperthermia and death. It's the reason we still need shelter even in a hot setting.

If nothing in your immediate surroundings provides shade and you realize you'll need to rig your own shade, make sure to allow air channels to funnel breezes through your space. Shade with no ventilation creates an oven.

John Wayne rides off into the desert in *Legend of the Lost* (1957).

If there are trees around or anything tall enough to cast a shadow, your work is going to be light. Just be prepared to move throughout the day to remain in the shade. You might need to build a canopy or dig into the ground to create your own shade. If you have a vehicle, you can stay on the shaded side, but remember that the shade will completely disappear for a while when the sun is at its apex.

Your first layer of shade will be your clothing. It is preferable to have long sleeves, long pants and a hat on a hot day to prevent sunburn, blistering and potential dehydration.

Once you've done all you can about clothing, hydrate as much as you can and, just as with the ice, do not save or ration your water. Drink it as soon as you need it and try to find more.

WATER
If you can find a water source, you've hit the jackpot, as this will considerably lessen your load for cooling. If the water is deep enough, you can immerse yourself and stay cool that way. **There are several considerations to keep in mind once you find this essential life-sustaining resource, so don't dive in just yet:**

- If you don't know how to swim, do not get in.
- If there is a current, do not get in.
- If there are predators in the area, do not get in.
- If there is known harmful bacteria in the water, do not get in.

Even if any of the above are present, you can still cool yourself down by splashing water onto your head and torso and letting the air facilitate evaporative cooling. If you find a shallow stream, you might try getting in and laying down. You'll want to be diligent in checking yourself for leeches afterward, so decide ahead of time whether that's something you're mentally and physically equipped to deal with before wading in. Wearing wet clothes on a breezy day will also produce efficient cooling.

REST
It may sound counterintuitive to those who take pride in being productive, but rest is the key to cooling down and staying comfortable. When you find or make that shady spot, rest in the breeze while the sun shines hot.

If you can arrange it, the combination of water, rest, shade and breeze will keep you comfortably cool. If you are in a very hot climate, you might consider reversing your days and nights: Sleep and rest while the sun shines, then do your moving around and working at night when it cools off. In a dry climate, resting during the hottest part of the day not only keeps you cool but also conserves your hydration. You don't want to work and sweat unnecessarily unless you have all the potable water you need to replenish your vital volume. Dehydration leads to hyperthermia, which can lead to heatstroke and death, so use your body's need for rest to your advantage.

SHELTER

ONE OF the first things to consider when you find yourself in the wild is how you'll keep the elements away. There are several different types of shelters that can be constructed in the wild. Choose one that can be made efficiently with the resources available, but also be sure that it's the best choice for providing protection from the elements.

Only make your shelter as large as it needs to be. Your body will warm a small space. Digging a runoff channel will help keep you dry. A lean-to is the best choice of natural shelter. Maintain a fire 5 feet from the opening, close enough to keep you warm and dry but far enough away that your shelter isn't at risk of catching fire. Choose a natural windbreak or create one. Cold ground conducts heat away from your body. Pad your sleeping space with leaves, boughs, pine needles, moss or any other material you can collect.

John Wayne and Elsa Martinelli in *Hatari!* **(1962).**

QUESTIONS TO ASK YOURSELF WHEN SELECTING A SHELTER SITE

- Is there enough material in the immediate vicinity to construct what I need?
- Is the space big enough for me to lay down?
- Is the ground level?
- Is it close to a signaling site?
- Is it close to a water source?
- Is it free from bugs and snakes?
- Is there protection from wild animals, falling rocks, trees and limbs?
- Can this site flood?
- Is there any danger from rising water, running water or avalanches?
- Can I make a fire close enough to keep me dry and warm?

The rule of thumb is to build it up about 18 inches high. When creating shingling for your shelter, lay the "tiles" in an overlapping fashion that causes rainwater to run off of, not into, the shelter.

TENTS

In your best-case scenario, you will have a manufactured tent and be able to stay protected from the elements. Tents come in many sizes, from one-person shelters to 20-person outposts. Your tent is your shelter, your home away from home. If you are going to invest in a tent, you have a few choices to make. How big do you want it to be? Do you want it to blend in or stand out? Do you want to be able to stand up in it? Do you plan to sleep on a cot or on the ground? Do you want it to have a vestibule or outer chamber for gear and shoes? How many people do you

(continued on page 182)

HOW TO MAKE A LEAN-TO

Follow these steps to construct this basic shelter:

1. Cut two stout sticks. If you can find sticks that are already bifurcated (one branch that splits into two or more), you can use those as anchor points. If not, straight sticks will do as long as they are strong and roughly 4 feet long.

2. Cut a third stick, about 6 feet long. This will be the ridge line of your "roof."

3. Plant the two stout, bifurcated sticks into the ground by the single end roughly 5 feet apart. If you were not able to find any bifurcated sticks, you can choose four straight sticks and plant them at angles to cross at the top like an X. The X takes the place of the bifurcation.

4. Lay the 6-foot stick across the tops (bifurcated or X ends) of the two sticks you planted and lash them together for stability.
5. Gather plenty of good-sized sticks, limbs and branches. To make the remaining wall, place the sticks against the frame at a 45-degree angle. You should immediately see the lean-to shape.
6. If you have a poncho liner, use it to cover the wall you created and stake down the corners. If not, pile on plenty of leaves and pine needles until the wall is well covered.
7. Pad your sleeping space with leaves, boughs, pine needles, moss or any other material you can collect. The rule of thumb is to build it up about 18 inches high.
8. Ensure that your fire pit is 5–6 feet in front of the opening to keep you warm at a safe distance with no risk of setting your shelter on fire.

PLACING the roof material of your lean-to in an overlapping fashion will ensure everything the structure's designed to protect stays dry. You may want to test this as you build by pouring water on the roof.

STACKING the "floor" material of your lean-to ensures you're not lying directly on the ground. In the event of rain, this plush bedding will keep you from having to get cozy in a puddle of mud, so collect as much as you can.

want it to accommodate? How lightweight do you need it to be? How durable does it need to be considering the historic weather events of your region? How long will you be using it? Does it need to be carried by one person or can its components be divided amongst a group to be carried? If it gets damaged, is it repairable?

Your answers to these questions will help you narrow down your search considerably. If you are looking for a tent for a family, you also have the option of multiple tents for subgroups or individuals. One-person tents pack down quite small and are reasonably lightweight. You might consider a mix of tents and hammocks with mosquito netting and awnings for sleeping arrangements. If you plan to sleep in a hammock, try it out before you're in the middle of the woods. You might find you need a certain kind of pillow for neck support or a certain temperature-rated sleeping bag for your climate.

HOOCHES

Hooch is a word used to describe a quickly erected shelter made of a poncho. When spread out, a poncho is quite sizable. Having the ability to string one up can mean access to a quick place to get into shade or out of the rain. You can use paracord or bungee cords to put up your hooch. Bungees are quicker but you are limited in desolate areas by their elastic limits to the outer reach of their ability to stretch. If you will be in a heavily forested area, you are likely safe with bungees. You will need to be able to find four trees close enough to each other and in the general layout of a square. The poncho has a hole for your head and a hood in the middle. You will need to start by tying that closed. The best way to do that is to create a gooseneck by twirling the hood closed, bending it in half back on itself and tying it up that way. This will keep water out. If your poncho has grommet holes at the corners you can attach a bungee hook to one hole and then to a tree. If it doesn't have grommets, pick a rock or a small handful of dirt and put it on the poncho about 6 inches or so from the corner. Wrap the fabric around it and tie a piece of string or paracord around it. You have just created an anchor point. Either way, string all four corners up to the four trees you chose at a height that works for you to spend time underneath. If it is raining, you can find a 6-foot-long tree branch and use it as a tent pole, propping the middle of the hooch up high to let the rainwater run down and off all four sides. If your trees are farther apart than bungees can accommodate, use paracord. You will have to tension each line yourself to make the poncho taut but you have more flexibility for filling the space between trees with paracord since it's not cut to any specific length.

TARPS

If you have the option to carry a tarp, you will not regret it. A tarp is a multi-tool that has many survival uses. You can make a tent out of a tarp. A tarp can be used as ground-proofing under your tent to keep you dry if it rains. You can make a quick shelter just like a poncho hooch out of a tarp. You can drag an injured person to safety on a tarp. You can package a patient for evacuation. You can wrap up in a tarp for added

(continued on page 187)

QUESTIONS TO ASK YOURSELF WHEN SELECTING A SHELTER SITE

- How much time and effort will be required to construct a suitable shelter?
- Will it protect me?
- Do I have the tools I need, or can I make them?
- Are there enough materials?
- Can I modify an existing structure or natural shelter to suit my needs?

HOW TO MAKE A HOOCH

The Tent-Adjacent Shelter

A hooch is a quickly erected shelter made with a poncho. When spread out, a poncho is quite sizable. Having the ability to string one up can mean access to a quick place to get into shade or out of the rain. You can use paracord or bungee cords to put up your hooch. Bungees are quicker but you are limited in desolate areas by their elastic limits to the outer reach of their ability to stretch. If you're in a heavily forested area, you're likely safe with bungees. You will need to be able to find four trees close enough to each other and in the general layout of a square.

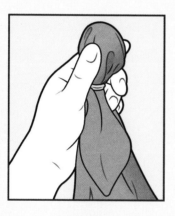

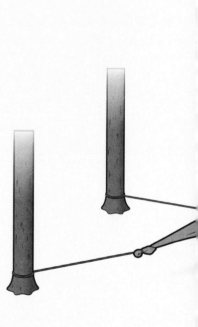

1. The poncho has a hole for your head and a hood in the middle. You will need to start by tying that closed. The best way to do that is to create a gooseneck by twirling the hood closed, bending it in half back on itself and tying it up that way. This will keep water out.
2. If your poncho has grommet.holes at the corners you can proceed right to attaching a bungee hook to one hole and then to a tree. If it doesn't have grommets, pick a rock or a small handful of dirt and put it on the poncho about 6 inches or so from the corner.
3. Wrap the fabric around it and tie a piece of string or paracord around it. You have just created an anchor point you can use. Either way, string all four corners up to the four trees you chose at a height that works for you to spend time underneath.
4. If it's raining, you can find a 6-foot-long tree branch and use it as a tent pole, propping the middle of the hooch up high to let the rainwater run down and off all four sides. If your trees are farther apart than bungees can accommodate, use paracord. You will have to tension each line yourself to make the poncho taut but you have more flexibility for filling the space between trees with paracord since it is not cut to any specific length.

SEALING the place where the hood of your poncho meets the rest of the material means the difference between a dry shelter and a wet one. Make sure to tie it off tightly and readjust if necessary.

John Wayne and
J. Carrol Naish in a scene
from *Rio Grande* (1950).
Inset: J. Carrol Naish
and John Wayne in
Rio Grande (1950).

warmth or protection from wet conditions. You can erect a privacy wall. You can collect and transport firewood in it or cover your stacked wood to keep it dry. You can use it as a signal panel to get the attention of an aircraft. You can make an awning for a hammock. If it is waxed, you can use it to carry water. You can make a stretcher out of it. You can use it as a rain fly over your tent. A tarp can be converted into a sail if you have a raft or a small boat. It can be an improvised hammock or makeshift poncho. Tarps are worth their weight in gold because of their survival support capabilities.

CLOTHING

Remember, your first level of shelter is the clothes on your person. You can subdivide that by outer layer, middle layer and base layer. If the temperature allows, you can create a shelter for shade or rain out of your outer layer. Conventional wisdom dictates you survive out of your clothes, fight out of your gear and live out of your pack. For example: The pockets of your clothing should contain all the items that are meant for your survival like a fire starter, compass, knife, flashlight, paracord, signal mirror and whistle, duct tape and water purification tablets. These things need not be full-size. A mini flashlight will do nicely. A small section of paracord and 5 feet of duct tape wrapped around a pencil are just fine. Even a button compass will work. Place your weapons on your belt or in your jacket, fishing or hunting vest, coat or other type of outer layer. This will usually be a firearm but could also be a large knife. Your backpack should contain your tent, food and water, clothing, medical kit, fishing gear and morale equipment. That way if you have to part with things permanently or temporarily, the very last things you hold onto are the things in your pockets, which could save your life.

ALL HAIL THE TARP

One of the most useful tools in your arsenal isn't what you'd typically think of as a tool at all. With a bit of creativity, tarps can be used to create just about anything, whether you're looking to stay put or keep moving. Turn to pg. 190 to see how to make a sail, how to wrap a patient for transport and how to build a stretcher using a tarp. Just don't forget to convert it into a hammock once you've finished with all your hard work.

PROTECT FIREWOOD

BUILD A HAMMOCK

SET UP A RAIN FLY

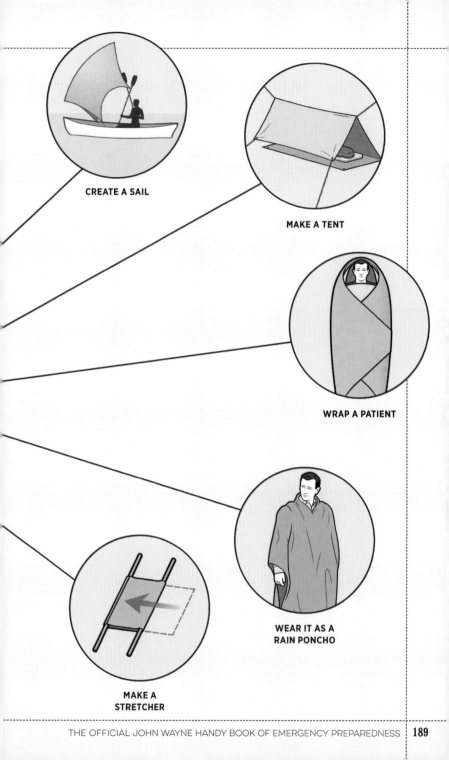

CREATE A SAIL

MAKE A TENT

WRAP A PATIENT

WEAR IT AS A
RAIN PONCHO

MAKE A
STRETCHER

TARPS THREE WAYS

MAKING A SAIL

1. If your tarp does not have grommets, use a knife to cut holes along two edges about every 10 to 12 inches large enough to accommodate your poles.
2. Cut two 6-to-8-foot sticks and weave them through the holes you cut into the edges of the tarp, one on each edge.
3. Secure the poles vertically on the left and right of your raft to allow the sail to catch as much wind as possible.

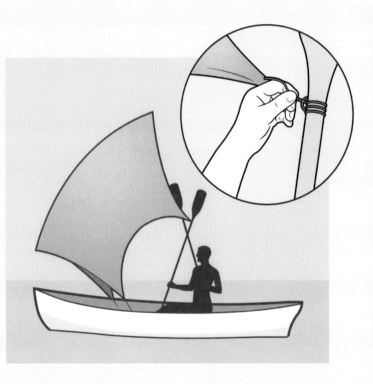

WRAPPING A PATIENT

1. If you have a sleeping bag, put the patient in, then lay them on top of the tarp as shown.
2. Wrap the bottom corner over their feet, then the left and right corners across them like a giant burrito. Use a belt, rope or paracord to wrap around them and secure the whole thing snugly in place.

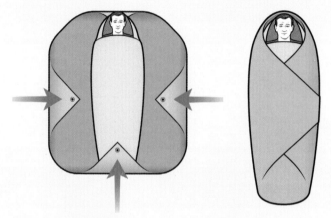

MAKING A STRETCHER

1. Lay the tarp out flat on the ground. Choose two sturdy and long (longer than the patient if possible) sticks or tree limbs for poles. Lay one pole across the tarp about one-third of the way from the left edge. Fold the left third of the tarp over the left pole toward the center.
2. Lay the second pole across the tarp on top of the now doubled material and about 3 feet from the first pole. Fold the right third of the tarp over the right pole toward the center. Place the patient on the stretcher and lift using 2 to 4 people.

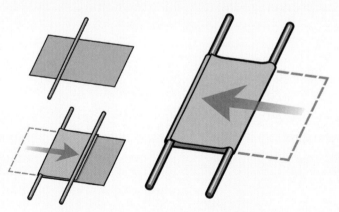

John Wayne in
Three Faces West
(1940).

DISASTERS

SURVIVAL HACKS, TIPS AND TRICKS FOR ENDURING JUST ABOUT ANY WORST CASE SCENARIO

DISASTERS

ATASTROPHES HAPPEN, and not just in the movies. War, famine, drought, pandemic, volcanoes, hurricanes, nuclear fallout, radiation, power grid failure, blizzards, civil unrest, coups—the list goes on, and none of them seem outside the realm of possibility in the modern world. We are long past the days of thinking it can't happen here or now or to us. It can. It does. That doesn't have to be the end of our story. If we understand what various types of disasters can do, we can also take measures to be prepared to handle what comes.

There are two primary categories of preparation: readying your capabilities and your stores. The former is done through learning, training, researching, studying and practicing the things you want to be able to do. The latter is achieved by accumulating gear, food, water, medical supplies and all other sorts of provisions. Both are needed well in advance of the disaster to position yourself in forward center of gravity (CG).

Almost every category of disaster threatens the purity and drinkability of your tap water. If you have advance notice of a disaster forming or heading your way, fill up all your bathtubs and any empty containers with water before pipes burst or toxic waste mixes with the water supply. Be prepared to cut back on your water use: take sponge baths and manually fill toilets with the water from your full bathtubs. If you get caught unaware, be sure to boil, filter or purify water before ingesting it.

Every kind of disaster will require you to make a protracted number of complex decisions. Stack the deck in your favor by doing some research and locking in a few premade decisions. Go through the list of possible disasters in the following pages and

walk through some if-then scenarios: If this scenario happens, then I will take that course of action. Know the layout of your area and your options for evacuation in terms of methods, routes and directions. Understand concepts like which direction the prevailing winds blow in your area and the fact that water flows downhill. These fundamentals form the foundation of your decision-making ability. Knowing your go-tos in various situations will help you manage your stress levels by giving you a predetermined way out.

HURRICANES

URRICANES ARE somewhat common (whether you live directly on the water or not), and it seems every summer brings a new "storm of the century." One of the best things we can do when faced with these storms is behave as cooperative evacuees, which means if local law enforcement issues a mandatory evacuation order, you need to comply. Thankfully, hurricanes tend not to move too quickly, so you might have several days' warning when such a storm is imminent. It's incumbent on you to take the following steps should the need to hunker down or flee your home arise.

ONCE YOU LEARN OF AN ONCOMING HURRICANE

- Determine ahead of time what your most prized possessions are, aka all the things you can't live without. Move whatever you can't take with you as high up in your home as possible to protect against flood damage.
- Pack all the supplies you'll need for your own survival and comfort, including a few changes of clothes, medications and medical devices.
- Bring anything that can be blown away by hurricane-force winds inside your home.
- Board your windows.

IF YOU ARE UNABLE TO LEAVE

- Keep plenty of dry goods and shelf stable food (dehydrated) on hand in case you have no refrigeration.
- Make sure you have enough bottled water for a week. If the pipes burst, you could get sick from drinking tap water.

Hurricane Wilma makes landfall in Naples, FL, on October 24, 2005.

- Keep a robust first aid kit to treat a wide variety of things including but not limited to cuts, impalements, burns, fractures and food poisoning, as these may occur during or after the storm.
- Once the hurricane has passed, let people know you're safe.

IF YOU ARE EVACUATING
- Shut off the water, electricity and gas.
- Take your pets with you.
- Pack and head away from the affected area as soon as possible to avoid getting stuck in traffic.

A neighborhood leveled by Hurricane Michael near Mexico Beach, Florida, in 2018.

A SERIOUS THREAT

There are several communities in the United States who, after more than a decade, have never regained all they had before a massive hurricane came through. Depending on the extent of the damage, the economy of the region, the attainment of federal aid and the resiliency of the people, some towns may never thrive again. A significant event like a hurricane changes people. Some come out stronger than before and some are destroyed. Hurricanes are always serious and even a "mild" one can kill people and destroy property. All hurricanes—especially those that are Category 3 and above—should be planned for and responded to with gravity. Stay updated on statewide evacuation plans and have a sense of the determined routes for making your way inland.

ONCE YOU HEAD OUT...

- Keep calm and maintain an orderly departure. Panic only breeds chaos.
- It's always a good idea to have a paper map of the immediate and adjoining areas as maps do not require batteries and do not fail. Study the maps and acquaint yourself with the local area, main arteries of travel, side routes and where they go and emergency services like hospitals, fire and police stations.
- Head inland, steering clear of high water, flooded roads and downed power lines. Pay attention to detours, emergency routes and travel changes.
- Listen to the radio for updates on road closures, detours, evacuation routes and hurricane shelters.
- Do your research about the crime statistics in the various sections of town and make sure not to risk getting stranded in a high-risk area.
- Once you're out of harm's way, let people know you're safe.

GOOD PRACTICES BEFORE ANY STORM

- Ensure your sump pump is working.
- Clear your gutters of debris.
- Cut down dead limbs from your trees.
- Trim your hedges/bushes.
- Ensure your roof is secured with hurricane straps. If your home is older, consider installing them yourself

TORNADOES

 ORNADOES ARE quick, fierce and fairly localized. Unlike a hurricane, which can take a week to blow itself out, a tornado packs a wallop over a short period of time. A tornado forms when a rotating column of warm air traveling up meets a rotating column of cool air traveling down. With the right conditions, the same storm can spawn several tornadoes one after another. If one just passed by, you might not be in the clear—there could be another (or a few more) forming behind it.

A whole section of the U.S.—from Texas to South Dakota and from Colorado to Kentucky—is called Tornado Alley due to how frequently it experiences tornadoes.

During a thunderstorm, keep an eye out: The sky may turn green and an eerie stillness may precede the funnel cloud. A tornado can sound like a freight train heading in your direction at full speed.

IF YOU GET CAUGHT OUTSIDE...

- Watch the sky. Run the opposite direction from the funnel cloud, then get to low ground. Lie flat on the lowest part of the ground, facedown.
- Open your mouth to allow the air inside and outside your lungs to equalize. Protect your head (prioritizing your ears) with your arms. Close your eyes. Cross your legs to protect your femoral arteries. Get as far as you can away from anything that can be picked up and thrown around by the storm, including cars.
- You can also swim into the middle of a body of water if it is safe to do so. Tornadoes jump over water, and this will give you the most amount of clearance as the funnel cloud jumps over the water.

A tornado spotted in Campo, Colorado, May 31, 2010. Inset: An aerial view showing the aftermath of tornadoes in Mayfield, Kentucky, December 15, 2021.

ONCE YOU LEARN OF AN ONCOMING TORNADO

- Taking shelter underground is your best bet. If a tornado lands directly on a house or any building, it will blow it apart above ground, which means you're better off underground. Get to a basement, bunker, cellar, storm cellar or storm shelter and stay put until the storm passes.

- Use a mattress to shield yourself from flying or falling debris, e.g., broken glass, shards of metal or anything else that might get loose in the storm. If you can't get underground, you'll want to get in a bathtub and cover yourself with a mattress.

IF YOU ARE OUTSIDE

- Look for an open area with very few trees around.
- Try to find a ditch, ravine, or other low-lying area and lie face down, protecting your head, ears and neck by covering them with your arms.
- Cross your legs to protect your femoral arteries from anything that might be thrown around by the storm.
- Allow the air inside and outside your lungs to equalize by keeping your mouth open.

FLOODS

F

LOODS CAN happen far more quickly than we envision and are remarkable in their destructive power and violence. The trick here is to avoid or outrun the water altogether.

Water, of course, flows downhill, so gaining high ground is going to be the key to ensuring your safety. The ability to move rapidly away from a flood is a lifesaver, which means you may not be able to carry a heavy pack.

Never go toward or into the water. If it blocks your way, turn around and find a new route. Six inches of moving water can knock your feet out from under you and 12 inches of moving water can carry a car away. It looks deceptively benign, sure, but even a light current is exhausting to fight and hard to overcome.

There are two primary reasons people drown in moving water. The first is exhaustion from fighting that magnitude of raw power. The second is getting pulled under or lodged under something that holds you down. Avoidance is paramount. Do not traverse a bridge over violently moving or rising water. If you are trapped in

IF YOU ARE IN AN AREA THAT HAS ANY RISK OF FLOODING, THERE ARE THINGS YOU'LL WANT TO KNOW IN ADVANCE

- Where is the water source with a flood risk?
- In which direction is it relative to your location?
- In which direction will the water flow if the volume suddenly increases?
- Which direction will take you uphill?
- Where are the edges of the floodplain (the low-lying area of ground adjacent to a river)?

John Wayne in
Circus World
(1964).

your car, stay inside: It just became your flotation device.
If you are in a building, get to the highest floor.

Remember: Water conducts electricity. Try to stay
out of the water and maintain awareness of anything
electrical in the vicinity.

BLIZZARDS

F BLIZZARDS are a possibility in your part of the country, stocking your house and vehicles to weather the storm in advance is critical. The important thing to remember with blizzards is that they can surprise us. Many times what was forecast to be a simple 6-inch snow ends up lingering in the area and dumping far more accumulation than could have been predicted. Occasionally, there will be a second storm right behind the first one, too close for radar to detect. If the conditions are right, an affected area may simply produce storm after storm in the same location.

Many medical concerns like frostnip, frostbite and hypothermia can be solved by focusing on doing everything in your power to stay warm. Keep plenty of chopped wood on hand for your fireplace, pellets for your pellet-burning stove and gas for your generator and vehicles.

The survivability of being caught out in a blizzard depends on training, supplies and mindset. Your car becomes your shelter and you can improve your odds of survival dramatically by stocking it with food, warmth producers like blankets, clothing and chemical heat packs and extra gas for the engine. You can use the car heat and radio if you have the gas. You can melt snow for water (just as you would at home). Staying dry and fed will help you stay warm.

Winterize your vehicles in terms of battery maintenance, fluids, tires, survival gear and medical kits. Keep your gas tank filled. Avoid driving in a blizzard at all costs.

If you need to go outside your house or vehicle for any reason, attach a rope to the house or car and hold it as you move around so you can follow it back to safety even when you can't see.

John Wayne in
The Big Trail
(1930).

IF YOU GET CAUGHT OUTSIDE

- Stay dry by taking shelter under any cover, such as an awning, an overhang or dense pine forest.

- Stay hydrated.

- Be prepared to hunker down. You can get turned around and lost in an instant in whiteout conditions.

- Keep your head and hands covered to stay ahead of hypothermia and frostbite.

AVALANCHES

NOTHING STRIKES fear into the heart of even the most seasoned alpinist like an avalanche. Untold tons of snow and ice careening down a mountain face can cause significant damage to structures and forests, which means they can easily batter the human body—and if the brute force doesn't get you, suffocation easily can. Though you may believe you'll never be in a position where you'll be contending with an avalanche, that's not how those using the forward CG mindset should think. The good news about avalanches is that in many cases they are predictable. The bad news is the ones you can't predict are the ones you need to prepare for. Can you prevent an avalanche? Not exactly. Can you survive one? Yes! Learn to read the signs before you go out on the slopes.

AVOID USING THE SLOPE IF ANY OF THESE ARE PRESENT

- An overhang of wet snow
- Recent cracks
- The shady side of the mountain
- Steep terrain
- Recent rain
- A recent earthquake
- A recent avalanche
- Hollow-sounding snow
- Wind coming from behind a snowy overhang
- Non-groomed rural roads and terrain
- A foot or more of fresh snow on a steep face
- Local knowledge that the area is dangerous

IF YOU HAVE TO TRAVERSE THROUGH A RISKY AREA

- Traverse the slope as high up as you possibly can.
- Never go there alone.
- Connect yourself by rope to your teammates and stay connected.
- Pay attention to weather conditions: recent, current and forecast.
- Plan a route that will take you as close as possible to large, solid objects like boulders and trees and stay uphill of them.
- Carry a cigarette lighter.

Make no mistake: Avalanches are killers. The best rule for all survival is prevention and avoidance (see next page). However, if you do find yourself overwhelmed by an avalanche, there are still ways to avoid its life-taking potential.

IF YOUR POWERS OF PREVENTION HAVE FAILED YOU AND YOU ARE CAUGHT IN AN AVALANCHE, HERE ARE THE METHODS THAT WILL GIVE YOU THE BEST CHANCE FOR SURVIVAL

1. Jump uphill of any crack that forms in your presence.
2. Move to the outer edge of the slope as fast as possible. The avalanche will funnel the snow down the center of the slope, trying to create or follow a trough. This gives you an advantage: Maneuver yourself out of this predictable path as quickly as you can through any means available.
3. If getting out of the way of the torrent of snow isn't possible, you'll want to ditch any and all superfluous gear to prevent impact injuries and puncture wounds and make your body easier to control in the snow. Kick off your skis, snowboard or snowshoes and let go of your poles and backpack.
4. If you get overtaken by the avalanche, and there's nothing to hold onto, "swim" parallel to the cascading snow almost like you're body surfing, in an effort to stay on top of it.
5. At any point during the avalanche, if you have a chance to grab on to anything you pass, like a tree or a boulder, take it.
6. Cover your face with your hands, then work to create space for a pocket of air by making your body as big as possible: inhale to inflate your lungs, spread your elbows apart and nod your head back and forth in exaggerated movements to create as much space for wiggling as you can. Next, spark a lighter to determine which direction is up, then begin to dig and, if possible, punch your hand up as far as it will go to create a ventilation shaft. Do not fight or exhaust yourself—conserve your strength until the avalanche has stopped, then use your energy to tunnel out.

FIRES

REGARDLESS OF whether or not you live in a part of the country where blazes are a seasonal threat, every fire begins with a spark. It can happen anywhere, and your ability to contain the threat can mean the difference between losing an item—like a frying pan—or your property in a five-alarm house fire.

IN THE EVENT OF A HOUSE OR BUILDING FIRE, YOU MUST MAKE CRITICAL DECISIONS IN A MATTER OF MOMENTS

- Evacuate immediately. Smoke can become incapacitating in seconds.
- Cover your eyes, nose and mouth with any fabric you might have handy to minimize breathing in particulate matter. You can use a wet bandana or washcloth as a makeshift mask. There are commercial smoke hoods you can buy that will give you about 10 minutes to escape.
- Close all doors to keep the airflow to a minimum.
- Lightly touch door handles before opening them to feel for heat.
- Close windows to starve the fire of the oxygen it needs.
- Get down and stay below the smoke.
- Make your way out and away from the scene.

TIP: Flames go up, so the worst part of the conflagration is likely to be lower down. Try not to trap yourself on a level from which you can't get out.

IF THE FIRE IS OUTDOORS

- Find a fire break like a body of water, paved surface, mud or dirt with no vegetation. Immerse yourself in water or get down in the mud or dirt. Low ground

like ravines or even ditches are best.
- Stay out of areas with anything flammable like grass or trees.
- Wait in place. If you've beat the fire to a fire break, it will either burn itself out or go around your area of shelter. If you have any choice in the matter, go upwind. The fire will move away from you.
- Wrap yourself in a mylar blanket, which will function as a temporary shield. It'll heat you up like a baked potato, but it can prevent your clothes from igniting. Afterward, you'll want to seek medical care for burns, smoke inhalation or dehydration. But at least you'll have made it through hell and back.

VOLCANOES

 HERE ARE certain places in the world where active volcanoes are a very real concern, whether you live there or are visiting. Here's what to do before, during and after an eruption to maximize your safety and odds of survival.

BEFORE

Do your research: Is your home or intended destination inside the Ring of Fire of the Pacific Rim, in Mexico or in the East African Rift? Have there been any known volcanoes in the area? Have any alerts been issued? If so, make sure you have the following on hand: N95 face mask (or smoke hood), flashlights, food, goggles that seal, long pants, long-sleeved shirt, medical supplies, radio and water. Prepare a bug-out bag (see pg. 14). Have a plan for evacuation.

DURING

Wear your goggles, face mask, long pants and long-sleeved shirt. Evacuate to a safe, indoor location. Take your pets with you or bring them inside. Have an alternate plan of evacuation that doesn't include motor vehicles or airplanes, since ash clogs engines and lava melts tires. Put distance and terrain between you and the lava flow. Note the flow path and take the high road since lava and water flow downhill. Be aware of irregular water levels and flow paths.

Once inside, keep all the windows and doors tightly sealed to keep out as much ash as possible. Turn off the environmental system and close all vents. Close the fireplace flue. Listen to the radio for updates. Stay hydrated. Tend to any open wounds or burns immediately to prevent infection. Remain inside until it's announced that venturing outdoors is safe.

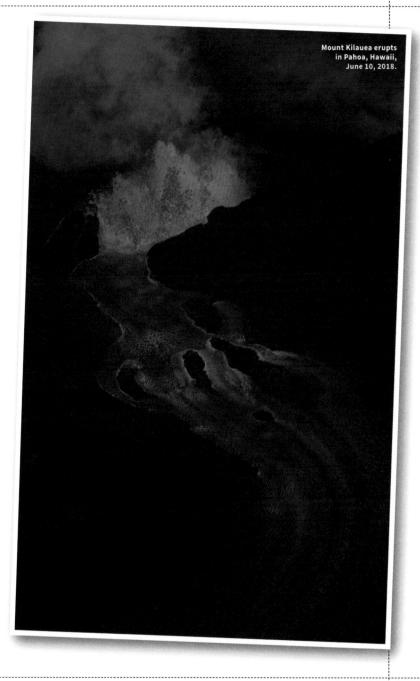

Mount Kilauea erupts
in Pahoa, Hawaii,
June 10, 2018.

AFTER

Seek medical attention. Alert your loved ones to your status. Make sure you are cleared before heading back into the affected area. Take care of your physical needs: eat, sleep, water, etc.

THE DANGERS OF ASH

It doesn't take a trip to Pompeii to know volcanic ash can prove deadly. Since ash clogs things like engines and lungs, face coverings such as N-95 respirators must be worn during an eruption to protect yourself from ash inhalation. When people die from a fire, it's usually due to the particulate matter in the smoke they inhale. The same is true for volcanic ash. Ash can cause a car or aircraft engine to fail can also make driving surfaces slick and dangerous. It can disable the environmental systems in a house if it overwhelms the air filters. Your ability to filter ash out and keep air flowing is key.

Make sure you have all the personal protective equipment you need when the time for cleanup arrives.

HOW TO TREAT THIRD-DEGREE BURNS

These severe burns can be life-threatening if they cover 9 percent or more of the body's surface. For treatment:

- **REMOVE** the surrounding clothing and jewelry near the affected area if possible but do not attempt to separate any material that has been fused to the skin.
- **CLEAN AND COOL** the area with fresh cool water for 30 minutes, irrigating the burn in a constant stream flowing away from the body.
- **COVER THE BURN** with burn gel and a loosely applied burn pad if you have them—if not, use a wet cloth. Do not impede circulation.
- **GET TO THE HOSPITAL** You will likely be transferred to a burn center.

Lava from the Mount Kilauea eruption encroaches on a home near Pahoa, Hawaii, May 6, 2018.

You will be disturbing and handling material that can interfere with your ability to see and breathe. Cover your eyes, nose and mouth and keep the outside of your filters (goggles and masks) clean. Do not attempt to walk or drive across cooling lava until it is completely cooled and solidly crusted.

The environmental effects of a volcano can last from months to years, so there's no absolute answer for how soon individuals and communities will recover. There is no point to cleaning and rebuilding until the ash has completely stopped falling, and that may only happen weeks after the initial event. Even when the ashfall appears to have stopped, it can start and stop again for weeks after the main eruption.

EARTHQUAKES

 ARTHQUAKES STRIKE without warning and can occur almost anywhere in the world. They range from barely perceptible to disastrous. You could be in any situation or setting when they hit but there are some fundamental principles to follow regardless of where you are.

- Stop moving and get down as low as you can.
- Hold on to something solid.
- If you are in bed, turn face down and cover your head and neck with your pillow.
- If you are indoors but not in bed, take cover in a door frame or under a table and hunker down low. Keep your face and head as protected as possible from falling debris.
- If you are outdoors, stay away from buildings.
- If you are driving, pull over and stop.

Depending on your location, a secondary problem might include the opening of sinkholes. If you are coastal, there may be a tsunami. Aftershocks can occur anywhere. A whistle is a good everyday carry item: If you find yourself trapped, whistles are louder and travel farther than your voice. You can keep blowing on a whistle long after you've gone hoarse from hollering.

Stay calm. Do not enter a building in the aftermath of an earthquake until you are professionally assured of its structural integrity or you could put yourself in harm's way.

Destroyed homes in the aftermath of the Loma Prieta earthquake in San Francisco, California, October 17, 1989.

LANDSLIDES

A landslide is the sliding down of a mass of earth, rock or debris from a mountain or cliff. This can happen on any sufficiently steep slope anywhere in the world for multiple reasons like heavy rain, snowfall, snowmelt, erosion, earthquakes, volcanoes or even human disturbances like blasting with dynamite. Rain loosens the earth, predisposing it to separate. Significant vibrations do the same. Gravity does the rest. Avoid places where this can happen. If worst comes to worst and you become aware that a landslide is taking place, escape it by climbing above it. If you are inside a structure, close the uphill windows and open the downhill windows to prevent the accumulation of debris and allow what has already accumulated to escape.

CHEMICAL SPILLS

UEL AND oil are the types of chemical spills that seem to get the most media coverage; however, chemicals come in the form of solids, liquids or gas. People and wildlife can die from inhaling poisonous gases or coming into contact with chemical solids or chemical liquids. Water becomes contaminated. The ecosystem suffers a blow and struggles to sustain life. Since we have the capability to transport hazardous material across vast expanses of land and sea, these disasters can happen anywhere. We see it in overturned trucks, derailed trains, and cargo (container) ship accidents.

There's not a lot anyone can proactively do when faced with a sudden release of highly toxic chemicals beyond evacuating the area as soon as possible. Don't linger and avoid touching or otherwise coming into contact with the substance if you can.

As you head upwind, constantly check your surroundings—you don't want to rush into an area where multiple people are down. Stay back and call out to them from a distance. Throw something they can grab onto and pull them to safety.

Brush dry chemicals off your person in a direction away from your body. Wash wet chemicals off in the same direction. Do your best not to breathe in the chemicals. Don protective equipment like a mask, glasses/goggles and gloves. In the current environment of COVID-19, almost everyone has a mask. Any kind of glasses will help to some extent, even reading glasses. You are simply trying to protect yourself from suffering further damage as you interact with the chemicals. Swim goggles, motorcycle goggles and ski goggles

Evidence of toxic waste dumped at Love Canal, a neighborhood in Niagara Falls, New York, May 23, 1980.

will all work, as will latex gloves, dishwashing gloves, gardening gloves and rappelling gloves. If you have any of these, put them on right away. If you don't have them, get away from the area as quickly as possible.

If this happens indoors, get outside as soon as you can. Remove any sources of ignition in case the chemicals are flammable. Turn off the heat and the gas. Close windows and vents. Treat unknown or harmful chemicals like poison. Do not handle, breathe or ingest them unnecessarily. Put some distance between yourself and the affected area in case there's an explosion. Call for help. Keep all other people and animals out of the impacted zone. Seek medical treatment for burns or poisoning.

BIOLOGICAL CONTAGION

 E ARE already dealing with a global pandemic and have learned a great deal through this experience. Biological contagions can be bacterial, fungal or viral in nature. Such events can occur naturally or be man-made, whether accidental or as a result of terrorism. The results can be asymptomatic, allergic or deadly. Staying isolated from the problem area is your best bet for survival.

- Personal protective equipment is a must-have.
- If you are unsure of your own exposure, be prepared to seek higher medical care.
- If you are unsure of another person's exposure, keep your distance from them.
- Listen to the radio for updates and information.
- Keep your doors and windows closed, locked and even sealed until you know what your options are.
- If you know you've been exposed, isolate yourself until you understand what you're dealing with and what you need to do.

Americans no longer have the luxury of thinking of a pandemic as a far-off historical event like the 1918 Spanish Flu. By paying attention to national and local updates and taking every possible measure to protect your household, that heightened awareness will serve you well.

An illustrated rendering of the coronavirus cells that cause COVID-19.

BEFORE YOU TRAVEL

In recent years, we've seen a number of diseases ravage various corners of the world. From COVID-19, monkeypox and Ebola to persistent, well-known threats like polio, tuberculosis, malaria, dengue fever, rabies, measles, scabies, hepatitis and cholera, illness can be found just about anywhere. And this is far from a comprehensive list. For these reasons and more, if you plan to travel, make time to see a travel medicine specialist and get vaccinated against the things you are likely to encounter at your destination(s) and along the way. Whenever going abroad, going somewhere remote or going away from home for extended periods of time, be sure to pack over-the-counter and prescription medications to treat food poisoning, ear infections, flu and other common maladies.

RADIOLOGICAL/ NUCLEAR FALLOUT

 O LONG as there are nuclear weapons, people will need to consider what could happen in the event said weapons are launched in an attack. Existential threats can, however, come from within: As we've seen with the Chernobyl and Fukushima disasters (the latter of which was prompted by an earthquake and a tsunami), nuclear power plants can likewise prove extremely hazardous for the communities in which they are located should Mother Nature or human error cause a reactor meltdown.

Should you find yourself in either of those scenarios: When it comes to radiation exposure, your primary concerns are amount of exposure time, proximity to the radioactive agent and whether or not you've been shielded.

- Minimize the amount of time you are exposed.
- Maximize the distance between you and the radiation. Put as many barriers between you and the radiation as possible. Walls are good to start with.
- Go upwind.
- If there is lead anywhere around, get behind it.
- Go underground and seal yourself in.
- Change your clothes. Shower if possible, but be aware that the water may be contaminated. The goal is to get rid of any affected particles present on your clothes and body.

Radiation sickness (also known as radiation poisoning) can produce loss of appetite, fatigue, fever, nausea, vomiting, diarrhea and possibly even seizures and coma. These can last for hours or months. Potassium iodide is used to combat radiation poisoning and is available over the counter. Be aware that it can be harmful and even fatal if taken incorrectly or overdosed, so be sure to read the directions carefully before ingesting.

ELECTRICAL GRID FAILURE

F THE grid goes down, you'll effectively move backward to a time of pre-industrial capabilities. Blackouts—such as the massive northeast blackout of 2003 (pictured at right), which affected 50 million people—have given us a taste of just how difficult modern life can be without access to electricity. A power outage can dramatically alter your everyday habits.

You'll need to be prepared to function in a way few of us have ever had to. If it is a simple widespread power outage, you'll still be able to drive your gas-powered vehicle. However, if it's the result of an electromagnetic pulse attack, even your cars won't start. Your cell phone will be useless. A devastating, wide-scale event like that would be either an act of war or an act of terrorism by a state or non-state actor. Carrying out an electromagnetic pulse attack requires a high level of knowledge, malice and resources.

There are plenty of people around the world whose lives would not be changed much by a lack of electricity. In modern Western society, however, these people are quite rare. Even the water running through our pipes and faucets is controlled by computers at the plant. The chaos that would ensue from a total grid failure is staggering. Imagine people whose lives depend on refrigerated medicine. Computer-controlled cars (1960s and newer) would not start. There would be no option for communication with anyone not in your immediate area. There would be no ability to harvest or transport food on a commercial scale. That's why it's smart to stock up on water, candles and oil lamps and grow your own food if you are able.

Manhattan as seen from the Brooklyn Bridge during a massive blackout in New York City, August 14, 2003.

If you have some prior warning, you can wrap your cell phone, laptop or other device in three to four layers of tin foil or place them in an old-fashioned film transportation bag (lead-lined). You can use an X-ray apron as well. These things will act like a Faraday cage to keep your electronics working, but once the electromagnetic pulse is unleashed, it's too late for prevention.

TERRORIST ATTACKS

ERRORISM CAN look like almost anything. It can be an act perpetrated by one person against another, a state actor or non-state actor, official or unofficial. At its core, terrorism is designed to get a person or entity to change its actions or position on something through the use of scare tactics and intimidation. Bullying technically falls into this category, which is how you can choose to view it. What bullying does on a small scale can be perpetrated on any scale up to and including the entire globe. Terrorists can and will use any kind of weapon to achieve their goals, including but not limited to chemical, biological, radiological, nuclear, electric, firearms, IEDs, grenades, suicide bombs, nerve agents and gas attacks, poison, kidnapping, hostage-taking, financial attacks, cyberattacks, land/air/sea-based vehicles or any other device you can imagine. By their threats, they rob their targets of their peace of mind and freedom of movement.

The best way to insulate yourself from the effects of terrorism is to be as independent as possible. If you rely on the public water supply, online banking and grocery stores, you're at the highest level of risk. The more you can act and move independently of those things, the more difficult you will be to manipulate.

If possible, try to have gold and several thousand dollars of cash on hand. Get a generator if you have your own well so you can use your own water

Firefighters evacuating a victim of a terrorist attack at the Bataclan concert hall in Paris, November 13, 2015.

CONFRONTING A TERRORIST

Only with training, equipment, the clear advantage and a plan should you consider confronting a terrorist. Having the high ground, outnumbering the enemy and having greater firepower are some examples of when to prioritize fighting back. If you can communicate with the intended victims and organize them into a unified response force—as the passengers aboard United Airlines Flight 93 did on September 11, 2001—you have better chance of disrupting the attack. If you fight, several of you must attack simultaneously and overwhelm your attacker by speed, surprise, violence, force and confusion. You may try speaking to the terrorist with a humble and surrendered attitude, but know that doing so could provoke them to attack. If you have a clear opening to escape, take it. Do not attempt to treat or rescue the wounded while your life is still in danger. Ensure your own safety before you help someone else to avoid adding another casualty to the mix.

SIGNS THAT INDICATE A POSSIBLE SUICIDE BOMBER

- Agitation
- Backpack or heavy-looking bag (may be concealed under clothing/jacket)
- Cell phone ready
- Clenched jaw
- Clothing that's inappropriate for the weather or setting
- Coat or jacket, regardless of weather
- Determined
- Freshly shaven body
- Fumbling fingers
- Hat
- Heavy belt
- Inability to make eye contact
- Looking around to an abnormal extent
- Mission focused
- Moving with a purpose
- Multiple layers of bulky clothing
- Nervousness
- Silent praying
- Sunglasses
- Sweating
- Vest
- Visible wires
- Wringing hands

source even without the aid of public utilities like electricity. Consider investing in home defense tools and familiarize yourself with long- and short-range firearms and training. Stock up on provisions so you can skip grocery shopping for months at a time. Make a safe place to go underground if there is an active attack like a bombing by creating your own shelter, bunker or panic room. If you don't allow yourself to be manipulated by fear and intimidation, you'll be able to keep some continuity in your quality of life even during a terrorist attack.

SPOTTING TERRORISTS

Obviously, a suicide bomber is in distress. They are in a crisis and are about to lose their life. Consider all of the emotional signs you would expect to see in such a person. However, depending on their personality, their signs may differ greatly. They may even appear relaxed, peaceful, resolved, unhurried and clear-headed. There are those for whom accepting their imminent death imparts a peace and tranquility that it will all soon be over. All their planning and hard work is about to pay off.

Remember to put the emotional signs together with the physical signs. If you see a person manifesting many of these signs, get yourself and your loved ones far away as quickly as possible. That individual may have already made their choices, but so can you. Survival is a byproduct of the action you take, so don't hesitate: act.

ACTIVE SHOOTER ATTACKS

CTIVE SHOOTER situations have become more numerous in recent years, especially in the United States. Schools, churches, mosques, synagogues, movie theaters, nightclubs, places of employment, concerts, sporting events—any place where people gather has become a target.

If you are concerned about being caught in an active shooter attack, prevention is, as always, better than response. Put your phone away and maintain situational awareness. Observe people and pay attention. Look at hands, eyes and facial expressions and process the data. Look for anomalies that stand out from the baseline. If everyone is in one particular mood or posture and one person is not, take note. Look for unexplained tension. Notice where their hands are and what they're doing. Are they in full view or hidden? Could they be hiding a weapon? This awareness might buy you the most valuable emergency preparedness commodity: time.

The average active shooter incident lasts nine minutes, and those 540 seconds might as well be an eternity when bullets are flying in your direction and you're scrambling for protection.

RUN, HIDE, FIGHT
Conventional wisdom dictates the best practice for responding to an active shooter is to run if you can. If you can't run, hide. If you can't run or hide, fight.

CALLING 911

Not everyone is practiced at resisting the urge to panic when connecting with first responders. Speaking in a measured volume, appropriate to the situation, can help produce calm. Be clear in your messaging. Slow your rate of speech and your respiratory rate to well below what feels right. Adrenaline will cause you to speak and act much faster and stronger than usual. It will also cause you to feel like everything you do and say is in slow motion. This is because your brain is processing information at a much higher speed than normal. That can create a false sense of needing to speed up. Resist that.

When you call 911, allow the dispatcher to take the lead in the conversation. They will ask all the questions they need in order to gather all the data they require to help you. Do not raise your voice or speed through your message. Answer the questions of who, what, where, when and how to the best of your ability. The question of why will be asked at a later time and isn't your job. Always ensure your own safety before making the call.

First, identify cover and concealment. Concealment is anything that obscures you from the shooter's view. Cover stops bullets—think concrete, vehicle engine blocks and trees more than 12 inches wide and 12 inches deep. Concealment is not an end goal, though—it's just a momentary shield. As you engage in your gathering, notice all the concealment and cover you can identify and formulate a plan on how to use it to escape the area. You can choose concealment as a stopgap measure to get you to cover.

When running, do so in short (3-to-5-second) bursts from concealment to concealment, concealment to cover, and cover to cover. There's a mantra you can say to yourself with every movement: **"I'm up. He sees me. I'm down."** In the time it takes you to say that, the shooter can reacquire you in their sights as a target. When you need to move from your current position, briefly stick your head out to see your intended path and possible options. Come out from behind your cover in a different place or at a different angle than the place where you stuck your head out to check your options. Quickly dash out from behind your cover and get to the next in the time it takes you to say that phrase. Do not run in a straight line. Zigzag your way in an unpredictable pattern. If you've found simple concealment, your first priority is to move to cover. You may need to move from concealment to concealment in order to get to cover, and you may need to move from cover to cover in order to get to safety. In priority order, your goals are to improve your position, get to concealment, get to cover and get to safety. If you can skip any steps, do it.

There is, of course, a time to fight. It requires total commitment and decisiveness. Use all the training and intellect you have. Get the people around you to help. Use whatever is in grabbing

reach as a weapon. Be aggressive and do not stop until the threat is no longer threatening. Survival will be a byproduct of your willingness to take action.

As soon as you get clear of the situation and to a safe space, check yourself over from head to toe for blood. If you find a wound, treat it, then call 911. If you're not injured, you are clear to call 911 right away.

A makeshift memorial in front of Pulse nightclub, Orlando, Florida, July 11, 2016. Inset: Friends of one of the Pulse nightclub victims gather in rememberance in downtown Orlando, Florida, June 13, 2016.

CIVIL UNREST

 IVIL UNREST can look like a coup, an insurrection or a riot. Even peaceful protests can turn violent if there is an instigator present. When the population is unhappy, everyone is tense. Leaders and politicians are desperate to be back in the people's good graces and improve their ratings. The citizens are worried about the economy or the infrastructure or the health crisis or education or freedom. Division sets in and social fault lines form, places where groups of people with varying agendas and worldviews rub up against each other, causing social friction and other tensions.

What might begin as citizens exercising their right to peaceful assembly could escalate into an all-out riot with little provocation. Panic, then chaos, ensues. This can make for a frightening, even deadly situation without proper preparation. But just as you would in an active shooter attack (pg. 232) or terrorist attack (see pg. 228), the objective is to escape the area as quickly as possible. If things feel off to you or if there are police gathering near the protest site, listen to your gut: Remove yourself from potential danger. See pg. 238 for how to position yourself in a crowd during a protest to maximize finding at least one escape route.

IF THINGS TURN VIOLENT...

Move fluidly away from the scene and in the opposite direction. Do not allow yourself to get caught between the protesters and the police, especially if tear gas or pepper spray is being used to control the crowd.

If the violence escalates and you can't get away from the crowd or the area: Stay on your feet. Bring your arms up to protect your head and create or maintain space to breathe. Hold on to the clothing, arm, hand, belt, bag or backpack of any person you're with to avoid

John Wayne in
The Dawn Rider
(1935).

getting separated. Come up with a quick
plan of where to meet if you do get separated. Try to
move to the back and outside of the crowd, then slip
out of sight and get to a place where you feel safe.

Become a hardened target. Make yourself a difficult
person to victimize. This begins with situational
awareness, but there's more to it than that. One of the
hallmarks of a hardened target is preparedness, which
includes having not only what you need, but the know-
how and discipline to use them effectively.

WHERE TO POSITION YOURSELF IN A CROWD

One wrong word or action can be all it takes for a protest to break into a riot. Know where to go and how to act should things go sideways.

- Whether you actively participate in or find yourself at a protest, do not allow yourself to be drawn into the center of a crowd. Stick to the outside perimeter and maintain a clear view of the group.
- If the group is moving, stay on an edge or at the back. Don't place yourself in a position where you could be crushed against a wall or trampled.
- Blend into the baseline around you. Dress the way everyone else dresses. Make it your mission to be ignored and overlooked.
- Do not become aggressive. Do not look people in the eye.
- Carry a bottle of half Maalox and half water and use it to rinse your eyes, nose and mouth if the crowd gets pepper-sprayed or tear-gassed.

IN A PROTEST SITUATION, EMOTIONS AND ADRENALINE ARE RUNNING HIGH. ANYTHING YOU DO CAN BE PERCEIVED AS PROVOCATION IF YOU AREN'T CAREFUL.

INDEX

PHOTO CREDITS

ABOUT THE AUTHORS

CHECK FREEDMAN is the COO of Captive Audience Prevention Training and Recovery Team. She is a graduate of SERE school and has implemented her survival skills in more than 20 countries covering six different environments: mountain, arctic, desert, jungle, urban and water. Freedman has been a survival instructor since 2013 and is a rappel master, ski instructor, technical scuba diver, bush pilot, self-defense instructor, Level 6 ASHI Emergency Medical Response Instructor and a Civil Air Patrol Search and Rescue Ground Team Leader.

Freedman and Jensen are also the coauthors of *Survival Ready: Life-Saving Skills and Expert Advice for Surviving Any Threat at Any Time.*

BILLY JENSEN is the CEO of Captive Audience Prevention Training and Recovery Team. He grew up in the Rocky Mountains and was a Boy Scout, Civil Air Patrol Cadet and avid fan of John Wayne. Duke's movie *The Green Berets* (1968) motivated Jensen to become an Army Special Forces NCO (Green Beret) with multiple tours in Iraq and Afghanistan. Jensen is a graduate of U.S. Army Combat Medic school, U.S. Army Cavalry Scout school, U.S. Army Special Forces school, SERE school, Jungle Warfare school and Anti-Terrorism Instructor school. As a civilian, Jensen is a Krav Maga practitioner and an ASHI Level 6 Medical Response Instructor who regularly teaches wilderness first aid, wilderness survival, orienteering and anti-kidnapping and hostage survival.

ABOUT CAPTIVE AUDIENCE

F YOU or your organization is planning on traveling overseas for the purposes of rendering humanitarian aid to any population in need, Captive Audience Prevention, Training and Recovery Team offers training at a variety of levels to maximize your chances for success while minimizing your exposure. Our training courses and services offer multiple tiers including pre-deployment readiness, crisis planning and response and post-incident help.

OUR OFFERINGS INCLUDE:

- Survival on air, land or sea
- Urban survival
- Desert survival
- Mountain survival
- Jungle survival
- Arctic survival
- Water survival
- Basic navigation
- Advanced navigation
- Personal protection
- Third-party protection
- Risk assessments
- Improvised weapons
- Found object fighting
- Mindset
- Combatives
- Restraint escape
- Evasion
- Surviving captivity
- Self-rescue
- Surveillance detection

If you would like to learn more about Captive Audience or are interested in participating in one of our courses, please visit our website: **captiveaudienceptrt.com**.

Media Lab Books
For inquiries, call 646-449-8614

Copyright 2023 Topix Media Lab

Published by Topix Media Lab
14 Wall Street, Suite 3C
New York, NY 10005

Manufactured in Malaysia

ISBN-13: 978-1-948174-66-4
ISBN-10: 1-948174-66-9

CEO Tony Romando

Vice President & Publisher Phil Sexton	**Chief Content Officer** Jeff Ashworth
Senior Vice President of Sales & New Markets Tom Mifsud	**Director of Editorial Operations** Courtney Kerrigan
Vice President of Retail Sales & Logistics Linda Greenblatt	**Senior Acquisitions Editor** Noreen Henson
Chief Financial Officer Vandana Patel	**Creative Director** Susan Dazzo
Manufacturing Director Nancy Puskuldjian	**Photo Director** Dave Weiss
Digital Marketing & Strategy Manager Elyse Gregov	**Executive Editor** Tim Baker

Content Editor Juliana Sharaf
Content Designer Alyssa Bredin Quirós
Features Editor Trevor Courneen
Assistant Managing Editor Tara Sherman
Designers Glen Karpowich and Mikio Sakai
Copy Editor & Fact Checker Madeline Raynor
Assistant Photo Editor Jenna Addesso

Cover Illustration by Richard Phipps. Photo Reference: Everett Collection

JOHN WAYNE
ENTERPRISES

1M-A23-1